# The Complete Cord Course:

*Working with Cords through Energy Work and Shamanic Healing*

## Mary Mueller Shutan

Copyright © 2015 Mary Mueller Shutan

ISBN: 978-1517235574

All rights reserved. No part of this work may be reproduced or utilized in any form by any means, electronic or mechanical, or by any information storage system without permission in writing from the publisher

Published by Mary Mueller Shutan
Cover Design by Mary Mueller Shutan
www.maryshutan.com

**Disclaimer:** The information in this book is given in good faith and is not intended to diagnose or be a replacement for appropriate medical care. The author is not to be held liable by any person for loss, damage, or difficulty due to the contents of this book. The exercises in this book are for individuals of sound mind, body, and spirit.

# Contents

## Basic Cord Work

| | |
|---|---|
| Introduction | 1 |
| What is a Cord? | 2 |
| Anatomy of a Cord | 8 |
| Basic Cord Discovery | 11 |
| Symptoms of Cords Needing Work | 12 |
| Where Are Cords Found? | 14 |
| Basic Cord Clearing | 16 |
| Basic Cord Cutting | 18 |
| What Does a Cord Feel Like? | 20 |
| Sword Cutting with Archangel Michael | 23 |

## Intermediate Cord Work

| | |
|---|---|
| Working with Cords to Significant Relationships | 28 |
| Working with Emotional Cords | 34 |
| Working with Cords with a Lesson Attached | 40 |
| Clearing Cords of Power and Unequal Relationship | 41 |

## Advanced Cord Work

| | |
|---|---|
| Introduction | 50 |
| How to Alter Cords | 52 |
| Tangled and Woven Cords | 74 |
| Cording to Places and Events | 85 |
| Cords to Spirits, Energies and Beings | 99 |
| Ancestral Lineage Cord | 106 |
| Cords to Past Lives | 113 |
| Cording to the Future Self and Destiny Line | 117 |
| The Midline Cord | 126 |
| How to Work with the Cosmic or Universal Cord | 132 |
| How to Work with Your Etheric and Astral Cord | 136 |
| How to Work with Your Mental Cord | 143 |
| Birth Cord to Mother and In-Utero Experiences | 149 |
| About the Author | |

# Basic Cord Work

**Introduction**

This is the basic course in cord cutting and clearing. It is intended to be direct and focused on understanding what a cord is, how it operates, and more importantly– how to work with them to achieve balance, health, and a greater state of clarity in your own life. Additionally, you will learn what it is like to have toxic, imbalanced, or out of date cords in your body.

The purpose of this course is simple– to introduce basic ways to identify cords in your own body and simple, clear-cut ways to remove these cords. This course is suitable for anyone who has an interest in Energy work, Shamanism, Spiritual Healing, or meditation, and can be utilized on your own or with clients and friends.

The release of cords can make a profound difference in our lives. It can bring us from feeling fuzzy, out of it, or in a constant state of emotional upheaval to consistently experiencing clarity, calm, and a more centered nature in our daily lives. Releasing, clearing, and altering cords to past relationships, past friendships, and past work and school relations can help us move forward in our lives. When we release energy, such as a cord, that entangles us to the past, we have more room to grow, more room to be who we truly are, and the opportunity to have more energy and vitality in our lives. Releasing or clearing cords to present relationships can allow for us to let go of past wounds or traumas, and to move forward in a healthier way with current relationships.

## What is a Cord?

A cord at its most basic level is an energetic connection between you and another living thing. Everyone that you have had a relationship with, even every acquaintance you have met you develop a connection, or energetic cord, to in some way. This cord allows for exchange of energy and emotions between you and the person on the other end of it. When we have a deep relationship with someone, such as family or partners, our cords become stronger, larger, and more complex. For example, we are exchanging energy and emotions much more with a family member than our waiter from a random restaurant we went to last week.

We have cords to every relationship and every acquaintance we meet. Many energetic and spiritual workers choose to look at cords as a negative thing, but they are not when they are in a state of balance. Energetic cords are vital to feeling connected and having a loving, understanding relationship. The connection during sex, the feelings of deep connection to family or friends, and the loving bond to a family pet are all examples of wonderful cords and cording mechanisms. These positive, or balanced cords can make us feel healthy, provide us energetic support when we are going through times of difficulty, as well as can allow for us to understand that we have a support network... or more basically that we are not alone in the Universe.

However, since we develop so many cords and have complex, and not necessarily simple, loving relationships, cords should be worked with on a regular basis, even the ones that are to people that we have a good relationship with. Cords that are to acquaintances, random people you meet, and people you no longer will be in contact with can simply be cleared and not be replaced.

Although it may not seem significant, we do develop cords to people we meet randomly such as store clerks, waiters, work acquaintances, people at the gym or grocery store, and other fleeting relationships that we may not think about. While it is distinctly more beneficial to clear one single cord to a toxic relationship, the hundreds of cords we have likely gathered from random and seemingly insignificant interactions over the years can cause for us to become energetically cluttered and mentally foggy. When we clear these hundreds of cords from insignificant encounters we allow for a great degree of clarity in our lives and our energy fields.

Cords to significant people and relationships can also be cleared to great effect. We may still have cording to past relationships, to family members or friends that we no longer talk to but once had a significant relationship with, to an old boss, or to a person from school or work that we no longer associate with, or do not care to associate with. Some of these past relationships may have even been toxic, abusive, or energetically incompatible. Many of our past relationships may have had an unequal exchange of energy– we may be giving away our energy to someone we have not spoken to for years due to a cording mechanism that is still in place.

When we have cords that are energetically incompatible it means that energetic exchange is intended to be equal through both sides of the cord in a balanced, healthy state. We are intended to give as much energy and emotion as we receive from our relationships. This, however, is rarely the case. Often we develop complex cords to people where we are giving much more than we receive– and we may find ourselves consistently drained of energy without knowing why.

We may also have at one point entered into a relationship with someone who is still obsessing over us or jealous of us (for whatever reason), and although we are done with him or her in terms of external reality (our day-to-day lives), we may still find ourselves thinking about them. This may be puzzling to us because we may not care about them, and we may find that we dream about them, visualize their face, or think about a past interaction that may seem meaningless on a somewhat regular basis. We may even question why we are thinking about someone, or why their image seemingly randomly pops into our heads when we don't care about them. If energetically sensitive, we may feel a surge of emotion or realize that this person is gossiping about us or thinking about us, and their thoughts may not be pleasant.

In this scenario the person is utilizing the past cord to send emotion and negative thoughts towards us, and this is very likely an unequal energy exchange– meaning that they are taking energy from you without your permission. If you were to clear this past cord, this person would not have an anchor or gateway into your energetic field, and their negative thoughts, jealousy, and the energetic impact of them would greatly diminish. It is also likely that the person will stop obsessing or thinking about you once you have cleared the cord.

It is also important to clear cords in your current relationships. This is obviously helpful for relationships that have a lot of baggage or trauma in the past, which will help you get a fresh start, but is also true of any relationship. As was mentioned, it is extraordinarily rare to have a relationship that has a "perfect" cord. This cord would be flowing with vital and strong energy, have equal energetic exchange, and there would be no resonant history of past hurts or negative emotions towards one another. While we all go through fights and even trauma over the course of a relationship, there should no longer be strong emotions or resonance as a result of such events. If there are, releasing these energies through cord work can be helpful to create a fresh start in your relationship. Even the strongest and healthiest of relationships can be helped by examining and working with energetic connections, or cords.

When a cord is cleared in current relationships there is an opportunity to clear out old emotions and your old selves. When we are in any relationship we grow and change, and we may be still relating as if we are a twenty-five year old in our relationship (when we first met our partner) when we are now forty years old. In that time both of you have become new people, but the cording mechanism that was put into place was anchored and created by your twenty-five year old self. By clearing cords there is a profound ability to let go of the past pain, traumas, and emotions of the relationship (as much as you are willing and able to) and to build a new cord that is based on your current emotions and current relationship.

It is important with continuing relationships to cut cords, not because you will never see them again or wish them ill, but to let go of the energetic exchange of the old cording, the past emotions and patterns that you no longer wish to remain of that relationship.

**Summary of the Purpose and Definition of a Cord**

So we have established that cords are basically meant to connect us. Connections can happen between people, people and animals, even people and places. Some of these connections are obvious. We have a connection to our parents, our best friend, our lover or partner. Some are less obvious or even wanted– the connection to our boss, to our in-laws, to the bully who used to make us cry after school, to the random store clerk we bought our new sweater from. Some of these we think about– how our relationship with our partner is going, or how our relationship with our father could be better. But many of these connections we do not put any thought to. The person you took a workshop with ten years ago, the woman you smiled at on the train, the people that you interacted with once or twice in your life you still might have connections and cording to.

    The good news about this is that you can clear all of these cords. The people I just described that you have interacted with once or twice often have a smaller connection, a fainter cord, than your mother or your partner. You may also have connections to people you have never met, past lives, ancestors, and all sorts of people, places, and things, you will not be able to consciously understand. But that is okay. The "random" cords (the people you have interacted with minimally) can be cleared quickly and easily, and will typically stay cleared. People, places, or animals that you have had significant or meaningful interaction with require either more clearings, deeper/more significant work to clear or change, or an ability to truly be ready to move forward and surrender the relationship.

    These random or less significant cords can be cleared through the basic clearing and basic cutting work. Even if you have a lifetime of cords from random meetings, these basic clearings and cuttings will clear these cords fairly quickly. For the more significant cords, or people you have had significant relationships with, these cords can be cleared through specific work with the cord, which is in the intermediate work we will go over.

**Anatomy of a Cord**

Cords can look and feel different based on your own unique sensing system. Some people see them visually– like strings, cords, or simply energy flowing between you and another person. Others can feel them in a part of their body, and this sense gets stronger when the connected person is in the room with them. Still others can hear, smell, or even taste these connections. Many of us have no idea and no sense of these cords at all. The idea of energetic connections, or cords, may only be vaguely familiar to you. Wherever you are in this process is wonderful. If this is the first time you are hearing or working with cords, or if you are a spiritual worker and energy worker with decades of experience, there will be benefit to both of you in doing this work.

The first way we will work with cords is to understand how they look and act for you. As mentioned, we all have different dominant senses. There is no "right" way to see or sense a cord. Rather than focusing on an arbitrary correct way based on my understandings and experience with cords, it is important to instead develop your own direct experience. When you have your own direct experience of seeing, sensing, and working with cords the work will be much more powerful than someone giving you their imagery of what a cord is and you simply replicating that.

Some cords may plug in your body, others may hook in, some may look like huge sewer lines, and others like bright lights or thin strands. Some may look like huge weavings or tapestries.

Do not doubt what you see or feel when we go through the exercises. It is important when you begin to do work like this to start to rely on your own judgment, your own sensitivities and psychic senses. You can be told what cords look like, but how you see or feel them individually through your own senses will be extremely important for how you end up working with cords, especially when you move on to the intermediate and advanced work. So start now, and determine that you will have an open mind to the information you receive, and however you sense, see, feel, even hear cords is right. Even if you get something "wrong" through your own direct experience when you work with this information on a regular basis you will grow in confidence and eventually be able to definitively state what a cord looks like or feels like which will be richly transformative for your life.

If you are unable to see or feel cords when you begin, that is wonderful as well. Continue with these exercises, and in time, you will be able to feel, see, or sense them in your own way. And by the way, these exercises work even if you do not consider yourself sensitive, or psychic, or even all that spiritual or in tune. Even the intention of clearing cords will be helpful, and in time and with some concentrated effort, you will begin to realize how you sense cords attaching in your body.

A basic cord consists of a hook or plug of some sort on your end, a string or cord that can range in sizes, textures, and shapes, and a hook or plug on the receiving persons end. This string or cord can vary greatly in terms of length, color, texture, and even shape. Typically there is a hollow in the cord, or some way for energy to be exchanged through the cord. This cord may be clear, like a straw, or contain a lot of residue or "toxins"- sludge type material in the cord.

The cord may have many layers with a small opening for energy to pass through, or it may have one layer and a large opening. It is more typical for insignificant relationships to have smaller cords, or straw-like cords with little energy leaving or coming in. It is also typical for complex relationships that have taken place over many years, or even decades, to have multiple layers, lots of gunk, and a thick cord with a distinct physical presence in your body. In some cases cords may be tangled, appear like weavings or tapestries, or even hook into other cords. These cords will be discussed more in the advanced section but can begin to be understood and worked with through the intermediate work later in this course.

Even knowing these generalities we may be surprised when we examine each cord individually that a cord to a boy that we had a crush on in fourth grade may be so wide and still so vibrant and filled with energetic exchanges and emotions, and the relationship to our partner may not be as large or dense as we might think. This is why it is important to have an open mind and truly explore each cord that remains after the basic clearing. This will allow for us to deeply understand how we interact with the world, and more importantly, understand who and what is impacting us energetically on a daily basis.

**Basic Cord Discovery**

Sit or lie down in a quiet space. Take a few breaths in and out. Now, let the thought cross your mind of a basic connection to someone you don't know very well. Maybe you are at a social occasion, a bar, or a PTA meeting. You see them from across the room, maybe they smile at you or you exchange glances briefly. You have both acknowledged that the other one exists, but you have never met before or even seen one another before. There is no real connection, spark, or sexual attraction between the two of you. Now, imagine that there is a connection between the two of you. This connection will extend from somewhere in your physical body to hers (or his).

- What does that connection look like?
- What does this connection feel like?
- Does this connection have a sound?
- Does this connection have a color, thickness, texture?
- Get as descriptive as you can until you are able to sense this basic cord

If you are not able to sense or see this, don't worry! It takes time. The more you work with this, the easier it becomes, and the more it will come into your awareness. This was just a start to understanding cords and how a basic, uncomplicated cord may look for you. If you can do this, you can go on to the next step. If you are having difficulty, simply sit with your body each day, doing a body scan (go from feet up to head, not forgetting the arms) asking for a cord to show up. Eventually one will, and this exercise will begin to make sense for you.

**Symptoms of Cords Needing Work**

This can again be fairly individualized, and it is overall a good idea, no matter how healthy and vibrant you feel (or how in disbelief you may be about the impact of cords) to do cord work on a regular basis. The number one symptom for most people of cord clearing needing to be done is fatigue without cause. We all get tired in our daily lives, but if you are experiencing fatigue without a valid medical reason, it is likely that cord work could be of benefit. This can present as burnout, such as a social worker, doctor, or someone who interacts with people all day feeling more drained than they should be after working. It may also simply be an overall feeling of being drained of energy, of certain situations or places causing you fatigue, or of coming away from interacting with certain people feeling numb, out of body, or fatigued.

Anyone who is sensitive, intuitive, or psychically aware should be working with cords on a regular basis. Nurturers, or those in care-taking professions also should be working with cords frequently. Both sensitives and nurturers are easily drained by others who take advantage of them by taking energy through cording. This is likely entirely subconscious– as people who are in a state of despair, need assistance, or are unwell physically, mentally, or spiritually are often grasping out with cords like tentacles or fishing lines hoping to bring anyone to them that can help them with their situation. Sometimes this is slightly more conscious, and someone specifically will drain anyone they come into contact with (or even entire rooms) by looking to and succeeding in cording to multiple people in order to boost their own energy. This is popularly referred to as interacting with an "energy vampire" and is unfortunately a common thing for empaths, sensitive people, caretakers, healers, and a wide variety of people to have to deal with.

    Other symptoms include feelings of strong emotion when thinking about someone, or when being around someone. This can feel like anger, fear, disgust, or any other emotion you can come up with. In severe cases, especially for empaths and psychics who are being corded to, cording can result in the transfer of illness, diseases, and emotions. This typically happens in cases of significant cording, or cords between a parent and child, between partners, or therapist and client. In the case of someone who is highly psychic they may be experiencing a wide variety of emotions, illnesses that strangely pass through, fatigue, and other issues that no medical professional can figure out partially due to cording.

Other physical symptoms include body pain in places that feels like a deep ache, a sensation of energy leaving the body, or even localized itching or irritation. Occasionally cords are toxic, and so heavily laden with emotions and unequal energy exchange that more disruptive symptoms can occur. These symptoms are typically localized to where the cord is inserted in the body, such as pelvic or lower GI symptoms when a cord is attached in the lower abdomen from a one-night stand or past relationship.

**Where Are Cords Found?**

Cords can appear anywhere in the body. Commonly they are in the chest, heart area, upper or lower abdomen, or really anywhere in the torso. Most cords tend to gravitate towards the midline (the center of our body) and towards individual chakras because of the energy and openness of those centers. It is important to know that cords can be anywhere, though. Many people who cut or work with cords do not realize that you can have cords from your feet, your genitals, your head, your back... anywhere you can imagine a cord can implant.

When we get to more complex scenarios, such as cording to places, other energies, lifetimes, animals, or even spirits, these cords are more likely to be anywhere in the body. Some of these scenarios will be covered in the advanced course. But basic human-to-human (currently living) cording is most likely in the midline, at the level of a chakra so it can easily exchange and sustain energy and emotion.

    Although cording is considered an energetic phenomenon, it is important to know that they do insert into the physical body. Although some of the less significant cords may attach to our lowest energy body, or the area directly surrounding the skin layer of our body, most cords are going to be hooked into the physical body and the energetic structures, such as the meridians and chakras, which run through and create the physical form. There also may be cords attached to the organs of our body, our spine, and the muscle layer of our body. Some of these structures can be quite deep, and cords can be inserted deeply or even off of the physical body (in our energy field), depending on the type of cord and who is on the other end of such a cord.

Now let's discuss what to do about cords. We will go from the simplest manner of cutting and clearing cords to the more intermediate, and generally from least time-consuming to the most time-consuming.

**Basic Cord Clearing**

Let us start with the simplest manner of clearing cords.
First, get to a place of relative quiet:

- Lie down or sit down comfortably
- Imagine a white light or sun surrounding you and feel it penetrate your skin
- Allow it to fill you up like a balloon with white light or sunshine
- Feel this full feeling throughout your body- from the tips of your toes to the top of your head, and down the arms
- Imagine this light or sunshine radiating from you- about six to twelve inches from your physical body
- When you are ready, simply say the words "I am filling with divine light. Any contracts, cords, negativity, or chatter surrounding me will be dissolved in this light"

This can be said internally or out loud. Feel free to change the language to suit you. The important thing is that you are filling up with light, and dissolving anything that is not light into the light of the sun. This will give the opportunity for cords to dissolve or clear away from your body. In fact, this basic clearing is not only good for cords, but is a good basic clearing for stress, emotions, and pain, and can be wonderful when you are feeling tired, unloved, or are having a difficult day.

This basic cord clearing can be used anywhere, at any time. It is the perfect "on the go" clearing and can be utilized every evening to clear away the events of the day, as well as any cords that you may have picked up during the day. Although it seems simple (and we as a culture have a tendency to believe that more complex things are more effective) this simple meditation done over time can clear out hundreds or even thousands of old cords from seemingly insignificant interactions over the years.

This basic clearing will also allow for you to focus on the cords that really need work. This means that when we clear cords, some of them we may not even need to acknowledge or know who is at the other end of them. We have not had a lot of emotions, trauma, or deep relationships to the people attached to them. In certain cases we have had significant relationships to who is on the other end of the cord and we are simply ready and willing to move on and so they also dissolve quickly and readily with the above meditation. When this clearing is done, especially after it is done daily for a week or two, the cords that remain will show us clearly what and who we need to work with.

The clarity that we can get from the above meditation can be quite profound. I have had students tell me that they could see more clearly (both psychically and physically), that they had more energy, and that they felt more of who they vitally were after doing it. Other people were able to see or feel the impact in their energy field. And still others, after doing this exercise successfully, were simply able to move on to clearing the more significant cording that remained.

## Basic Cord Cutting

Now that we have done a basic clearing, we can discuss a basic cutting. We will go over this basic cutting in two ways. The first is to imagine a sword cutting away the cords from the body. The second is to utilize Archangel Michael and his sword to cut away cords. Understandably, if your religious background does not include Archangels, the basic sword cutting will work, but do not let the fact that the second basic cord cutting calls on Archangel Michael stop you from trying it. Archangel Michael is traditionally called for this type of work, as he works with contracts and cords, but I would encourage you to see how it feels with him, or to call upon a deity, angel, or being that you feel would be suited best for this to help with the second section. It is important if you do change to a spirit, energy, or deity that is more suitable to you that you directly ask them if they are willing to work with and cut cords for you. Only proceed if the answer is "yes".

*Sword Cutting*

Again, sit in a comfortable place that is relatively quiet. Some people choose to stand for this because you will want to get both sides of your body. Do a quick scan of your body- starting at your feet and going up to your head, and feel, sense, or even see if you notice any physical discomfort, pulling sensations, or areas that feel devitalized and lack energy. If you don't notice anything, or aren't sensitive in this way, don't worry. This exercise will work even if you don't notice anything.

Now, in your mind's eye, ask to be shown your cutting sword. Imagine this sword in your dominant hand, and then allow for it to merge with your hand and arm. This means that you will initially view the sword as if holding it in your hand, and it will gradually meld, or merge with your dominant hand or arm so it is a part of you.

If you are not able to picture or feel a sword, or are not able to sense it merge, do not worry. Sometimes this can take a few tries to do, and you can continue with the cutting with your dominant hand with the sword separately being held even if it does not merge.

Using your "sword"- your dominant hand and arm- cut the cords of your body. Start by going about six inches away from your body, and sweep your hand and arm around your whole body. We talked before about how cords can be anywhere, so pick up each foot individually and cut any cords from the bottom of your feet, and make sure to do both the front and back of the body. Every part of your body should have the cutting motion done to it by sweeping the arm approximately six inches away from the body. There are areas of your body that you will not be able to reach with your sword. Just imagine the sword cutting through those areas, and do the best you can.

As you are cutting you may be able to see purple or yellow light emanating from the sword. These colors are showing the impact of the cutting of the cords and the change of your energy field. As you go over and cut again (I suggest going over your entire body six to twelve times when you do this) the light is more likely to be clear or a have a light, translucent quality to it. This exercise can be done as often as you like, but I suggest doing it daily when you are first learning it.

If you sense a lot of cords still hanging around, or want to take this cord cutting a step further, you can also cut closer to your body. Go one to two inches away from the body and cut again. This should clear up some of those more difficult cords.

After this exercise is done please go back and do the dissolution of cords through the sunlight method with the specific intent that any cords that have been cut fully dissolve. When we cut cords the hooks or ends of the cords are still likely implanted in our physical bodies. To fully feel the impact of cord "cutting" we need to go back and remove the root, hook, or implant that remains in our body. We can do this through the sun exercise with the specific intent that any cord roots remaining fully dissolve and clear.

**What Does a Cord Feel Like?**
This is a perfect opportunity to start to feel what cords are like. The best way to describe them is that they are a place that you feel stuck at– like there is something there. When you are cutting with your hand/sword, there will naturally be places where your hand

slows down, feels like it is going through molasses, or even stops. Chances are that those are areas that have a cord attached to them. Sweep over this area several times to make sure that you got them. If the cord does not remove, don't worry. It might just need more work to release. Again, this is a basic cord removal, so it is intended to generally cut cords. Our most complex relationships and cording will likely need more of the intermediate work, which we will come to soon.

    A few words about cord cutting before we move on… our logical brain wants to know where these cords come from, why they are there, and what the story is behind each and every one of them. I would encourage you for these basic cord cuttings to let that go. You don't need to drive yourself crazy knowing where or to whom every single cord goes to. Sometimes it can be important when you have a cord that won't cut with the basic cuttings or clearings to know this information, but for now, just simply cut away everything that can be cut. Let it go. What is important is that we remove energetic connections that are devitalizing us and that we no longer need, and that we will be more fully who we are and have greater clarity when we do.

    If you still have some cords after doing the first two exercises, don't worry. You did everything perfectly. Again, the cords simply need more advanced work. This basic cutting is intended for the random cords, people we meet once or twice, people we do not have much attachment or emotion to, and people we are willing and able to let go of easily. This is not to say that this cutting will not work for emotional bonds or cords that are to more significant relationships that you are ready to release. But, chances are, the longer you have had a cord, or the more significant the relationship, the higher likelihood that the cord will need more advanced work.

    If you felt like taking the sword cutting a step further, you can set up a word or symbol to "activate" your sword. Let the first word that comes to mind, or the first symbol that comes to mind, be your activation key. It can be as simple as something like "sword on" and "sword off", a Reiki symbol, or a symbol like a sword. When you are ready to do your cord cutting, say the activation word to the sword. If you are using a symbol, draw that symbol with your non-dominant hand into the sword to activate it. Do the same thing when you close. Say a closing word or draw a symbol to close. This will boost the effectiveness and let your body know when you are ready to cut cords. The more that you do the sword merging method the less you will need the initial imagery of the sword and the instructions to merge. You can simply say something like "sword on" or draw the image of the sword into your arm and hand and be ready to go.

**Sword Cutting with Archangel Michael**

Archangel Michael is traditionally thought to be who to call while cord cutting. He is an angel of protection and carries a sword of light. Traditionally, you would call on him to do the basic cutting for you with his sword of light:

- Come to a quiet space, setting up a white, blue, or pleasant smelling candle (optional) or simply close the door to your room or office to signify that you are starting a ceremony and do not wish to be disturbed
- Ask Archangel Michael to come in the room. If you have not worked with him before, this may take a few times until you feel his presence strongly, but continue knowing that this works even if you do not feel the presence, see blue or purple lights, or anything else you may traditionally associate with him
- When you are in a quiet, undisturbed space, take a few breaths in and out, getting a sense of the energy in your body, as well as the energy surrounding you
- Invite in Archangel Michael closer, and ask him to increase his presence and vibrancy in the room so you can really get to feel and sense him
- It may sound silly the first time you do this, but internally (or out loud) say "Archangel Michael, I require your assistance to cut cords. Thank you for any help you may provide"

You may use the following words to complete this sword cutting, or are welcome to switch the words to suit your individual purposes.

*I _____, call in Archangel Michael to cut all ties, cords, and contracts that are no longer of use to me. Please surround me with light so I can release anything I am willing and ready to. Please allow for your light to fully flow through me to release any negativity or negative energies that may be surrounding me or within me, either my own or from other sources. If there are any cords, attachments, or energies that remain, please let me become aware of them consciously in a gradual way that is helpful to my overall process. Thank you for your help.*

As I mentioned, you are welcome to change the words to suit your specific situation or pattern of speech. I always ask to learn things gradually because it often has a less detrimental or sudden impact to do so. We do not need to learn about all of our cords right away, or be overwhelmed by information about all of the relationships or energies that we are still corded to all at once. By learning this type of information gradually, and asking for it gradually, we can more easily handle releasing it and feel stable mentally, physically, and spiritually enough to do so.

After you do this, simply bow your head and allow for the light of Archangel Michaels sword to cut the ties surrounding you. If done right, there should be a palpable sense of presence or energy shift in the room. You should be able to feel, sense, or imagine light flowing through you and surrounding you as the contracts and cords are released.

Although this Cord Cutting seems complicated, once you do it a few times it becomes clearer and more powerful. The more that you use Archangel Michael as support, the more intense and clearing this is, so utilize it often. It is important when you end this work that you thank Archangel Michael for his work and release him– either by blowing out the candle or by verbally saying that you thank him for his work and you are ready to go about the rest of your day now.

Again, you are more than welcome to use a spiritual guide, angel, or being of your choosing instead of Archangel Michael in this work. There are of course many faiths and spiritual paths out there, and simply because Archangel Michael is well known for his sword of light and ability to release cords does not mean that he will resonate with your personal faith. The real ability to do true and powerful spiritual work is to choose the appropriate spirit helper for the task as well as one that you personally have a deep connection with.

It is unfortunate in modern society and spiritual work that we have developed a buffet sort of method for utilizing spirits, guides, deities, angels, and other presences in our work. When we develop significant spiritual relationships to a few energies, guides, or spirits, rather than attempting to contact a new one each time that we do work, we will find that we can develop significant spiritual relationships over time. It is by having the time and patience to do so that we can find ourselves truly immersed on a spiritual path, with powerful spiritual helpers, instead of continually swimming in the surface layers of the cosmic ocean.

If you utilize another energy or deity that feels more resonant to you, begin by asking them if they are able to do such a task for you. If they are able to release cords and contracts, get to know how they can do so, such as asking what tools they might use, or how they might like to be approached to do such work for you. Having respect for our spiritual helpers and forging a deep connection with them over time will allow for this work to rise above repetition and into your own direct and powerful spiritual path.

# Intermediate Cord Work

It is often the case that the basic clearings and cuttings we have gone over will get rid of a fair amount of cords and "clutter"- energies that latch and surround us without our conscious awareness. But it is also the case that several cords will remain after we do the basic, or more general, clearings. Let us look at the reasons why cords remain after the basic clearings and cuttings we have done:

- The biggest reason is that it is a significant relationship that needs some focalized attention as well as has specific requirements it needs to release or change
- You may be holding onto the cord subconsciously because you have fear, anger, or grief that is causing you to not want to release or even acknowledge the cord
- It may be a cord to a place, past-life, ancestral lineage, or natural cord that is part of your energetic blueprint. These scenarios will be gone over in the next section
- The cord may be there until you learn a specific life lesson or gain specific spiritual understandings
- A somewhat rare reason is that a person on the other end of the cord has some sort of power over you. This can be emotional power, energetic or in rare cases, magical. If you find that someone does have energetic or

magical power over you and you are unable to navigate the cord, finding an accomplished spiritual worker to help you can be essential

**Working with Cords to Significant Relationships**

By far, the biggest reason that cords remain after general clearings is because they are to a significant relationship.

*Why do these cords remain?*

Well, they are significant, and likely have been there a long time. We all have complicated lives, and most of us have complex relationships with our parents, spouse, sisters, brothers, long-time friends, and others. These cords are likely firmly rooted in, thick or dense, and contain a lot of emotions as well as life lessons. Quite simply, all of the past energies and history between the two of you make up the quality and energy of the cord created.

*How do we work with these cords?*

Cords to significant relationships are easy to spot. Quite often, they are in areas that we feel physical pain. If we have not done any cord work, we may not acknowledge that this is an energetic phenomenon, or something that can be improved by cord work. But chances are that any place that is significantly physically out of balance– meaning those chronic digestive issues, that feeling of tightness in the pelvis, and the pain we experience regularly in the solar plexus can be partially or fully because of toxic, out of date, or imbalanced cords.

So let's get to work! In a quiet space, take a few breaths in and out. Scan your body from the tips of your toes up to the top of your head (don't forget the arms!) and ask to see, feel, sense, hear, or in some way notice wherever a cord remains after your general clearing or cutting.

You may be shown one cord, two, five, fifteen, or too many to count. Pick the first one that really grabs your attention. You may want to rescan your body and ask your inner intelligence or gut instinct which cord you should work with first. Allow your focus to drift to that area of your body:

- What does that cord look like?
- What does it feel like?
- What colors, textures, and emotions do you sense there?
- How long has it been there?
- Can you sense who this cord is to?
- Get as much information as you can about it. If you cannot sense much, don't worry about it. Like anything, the more you do this, the easier it becomes. For this step, even if you get a vague sense of something there, such as a pulling sensation, feeling of heavy energy, or sluggish quality to the area you can continue

It may feel odd to ask these questions to your inner guidance system. I suggest allowing yourself to sense and describe the cord as vividly as you are able to, and then, as if you were talking to another person, ask the cord itself these questions. It is easy to not trust our inner guidance, or the answers that arise when we begin questioning these cords. Trust yourself for the time being as well as the answers that arise, knowing that you can always change your answers later, and the worst thing that could happen is that you simply need to go back to this cord at another date to work with it some more.

If you are blocking out the cord (you are not quite ready to deal with it yet), the area will feel blank, like a black hole, or like you can't scan it. The energy in this area will feel devitalized and there is often physical pain in the area. If this is the case, and you want to try to work with this cord, ask your body, and this area of your body a simple question:

*What would happen if I could see, sense, or feel the cord here?*

This simple question, most times, will allow for you to feel or see the cord enough to begin working with it. Occasionally, this doesn't work, and likely is an area you will have to go back to, or an area that will open up more when you work with other cords.

When you can feel, sense, see your cord clearly, gently ask the cord who it goes to. This may feel silly at first, but it works. You are beginning to ask the cord questions, like you would a person. With a strong visual, felt sense, or whatever sense you can get from the cord ask:

- Who do you go to?
- What emotions are here?
- What lessons are here?
- What would happen if this cord were cut or cleared?
- Ask any other questions that come up about the cord

The answers to these questions may surprise you. Listen to your gut instinct, the first answer that pops into your head. Do not argue or get discouraged with the answers. If you do not get an answer to a question, or get no answers at all, don't worry. Pick another cord, or simply end here and go back to this work another day. Even acknowledging that there is a cord there will begin to bring up formerly subconscious material so that you can work with the cord in the near future.

When you are ready, ask the cord:

- What would you need to be okay being cut?
- Is there anything else you want to say to me?

If you hear answers to these questions, that is wonderful. If you don't, try again on another day. When you hear these answers, and the cord says specifically what it wants or needs in order to clear or be cut, listen carefully. If you agree to it, agree and then in your real life DO IT!

For example, if the cord says it wants you to let go of anger towards your ex-wife, and that the cord in question is going to her, become aware of the anger you have towards her, meditate on ways to release the anger, or simply ask the cord how to release this anger. If the cord replies with specific ways for you to release this anger (such as a ceremony to release your relationship or breathing out your anger through your mouth) it is important to follow up on what it suggests. This means that you would hear what the cord has to say, let the cord know that you acknowledge what it is saying and you are willing to do it, and then go do what the cord has to say in your daily life. After the activity is complete, you would go back and again ask the cord to release.

Our relationships can often be complicated, and it is easy to second-guess the answers you receive until you develop a certain degree of confidence from doing this work over a period of time, but the palpable difference in releasing a significant cord should be enough to begin to convince you that both the answers you have gotten, and the work you have done with the cords, is effective and very helpful work.

When you hear an answer from the cord, if it is something you can do, and are willing to, you would agree. The important part of this is the follow-through. If you cannot agree, or it doesn't feel right to do what the cord suggests, even by you being aware of the cord and acknowledging what it has to say it is likely that the cord will be able to become more balanced. Simply revisit the cord when you are ready.

If you can, negotiate. In the same example, if your cord is held in place by anger to your ex-wife, and you are ready to release some of it but not all, say so. And then release it by again asking the cord how to release some of the anger. Even you saying so, or partially doing so will change the cord. And then you can revisit each time you are willing to release a bit more.

When you are willing to release some of the cord, or some of what the cord asks, simply take in a few breaths and imagine whatever needs to be lifted off coming out through your breath. For example, if the cord wants for you to release anger towards a person, and you are only willing to release some anger, you would at first say so to the cord. You would then gently take a breath in to the area that the cord is located and breathe out of your mouth, imagining a color that you feel is appropriate leaving your body through your breath. It is very likely that when you do this and then go back to the cord the cord in question will have changed shape or appearance in some way.

When you have negotiated or agree fully to the terms, and after you have done the suggestions from the cord, activate your "sword" in your dominant hand, and sweep over the area where the cord is. Fill up that area with white light coming in, or invite Archangel Michael to come in and cut the cord and fill it up with light. If you are willing, send light to the person on the other end of the cord by imagining their cord to you disappearing in the light.

You can now go on to the next cord you noticed, or simply take a few breaths in and out and go about the rest of your day.

**Working with Emotional Cords**

The next category is similar to the first in many ways, and you can certainly utilize the same exercise detailed previously for visiting with the cord and asking it questions.

In this cord category, the reasoning why the cord remains is strong emotions. This is an interesting category because the emotion may be about the person, such as detailed in the above example of the ex-wife, or may be a background of personal emotion that does not allow a cord to release.

Let us explore this further. A cord may not release because you are angry with your father because he was an angry man who abused you as a child. That cord will remain until you understand this cord, allow the cord to tell you how to release the emotions and what it needs to release, and learn the lessons behind the cord.

However, this can be complicated by your own personal history with that emotion. If you are an angry person this cord may remain because you have a background of anger as your base emotion. If your first emotion in an emotional, overwhelming, or traumatic situation is anger, the fact that you have an "angry" cord is both causing you to have more anger, as well as magnifying the cord.

This is difficult to explain, so let me give an example: a man suffered through abuse as a child from his father beating him on a regular basis. He has a cord in his heart to his father, which has the emotions of anger, fear, and the experience of victimhood in it. However, this man had also experienced anger from an early age and exploded with anger at every injustice he perceived towards him– from getting cut off in traffic, to family events, to the weather simply being cold outside. This is obviously a complicated scenario, but is very realistic about why cords remain.

This cord remains not only because of the relationship with the father, but also because it is feeding into the background emotion of anger that is part of his energetic makeup (and energetic field). It also likely the anger of his father passed down to him as well as the current anger of his father energetically being passed through the cord affecting him. Ancestral cord clearing will be gone over in the next section, but it is more than possible to clear these cords through the intermediate work– through the understanding and realization of the cord, the questioning of why it remains and what it needs to release, and then the action of doing so.

But for now, let's unravel this situation before I give the specifics about how to work with emotions and cords. This man has a cord in his heart to his father. The reason this cord didn't clear from general clearings is that it had a lot of emotions tied to it, it was a significant relationship, there were lessons to be learned (gone over in the next category), and it fed into his base emotion of anger that served him in some way.

This anger was not only from this cord, but also from many situations in his life, and the cord was simply giving this anger fuel. If he were to let this cord go, the anger would not be fueled as much. This is obviously a wonderful thing, but sometimes emotions make us feel strong, even if they are destructive. It takes a person really willing to move forward and to heal who is willing to let go of cords such as this and to experience the fear that is likely behind the emotion of anger.

When he checks in on this cord, the cord says to release he needs to forgive himself for not standing up to his father and protecting his mother, and that he needs to release his anger. The cord goes on to say that the anger is at himself for having to deal with this while everyone else got a normal childhood. He feels cheated out of a childhood and loving parents. When he feels this anger in his heart, he realizes that it is also covering up fear. That small child needs to know that everything is okay.

When this man works on this, he is able to recognize the anger, the fear, the small boy who is afraid, the yearning to have a normal childhood. The cord starts to change even with that understanding. Gradually, with working with this cord over time and revisiting it regularly for a few months, he realizes that he always is angry about being a victim, and that he feels abused at his job and in his relationships in the present day the same way that he did from his father. From this awareness the cord begins to change. Finally, the cord was able to release by the man forgiving himself for not standing up to his father. He was then able to cut the cord.

After six months of doing this cord work, the cord gradually shifted and changed and released bit by bit. The little boy who was so angry and scared was able to release the cord, shifting his entire energetic makeup of anger, fear, and reaction, to a quieter and less angry disposition. The understanding of this "toxic" cord and how it made up his identity and current life situation came to his awareness through sitting with the cord, being aware of it, and asking what it needed. Over time, he realized that it had a huge effect not only at the energetic level of a single relationship with his father, but at how he interacted with the world, and who he was as a person.

So, how did he do this? With a lot of work, and visiting the significant cord over time. But, here are the steps to working with emotional cords. You may always do the general cord "talking-to" that we went over in the previous category as well.

*Emotional Cord Cutting*
- Sit in a quiet place, take a few breaths in and out
- Scan the body, looking for cords that are emotional in basis. You can do this by asking cords that are emotionally based to come up, or just assume that any cords that remain that were not cleared by the basic cord cuttings and clearings likely have some emotions attached to them that will need some work
- When you find one, feel that area of your physical body that the cord is connected to. What does it feel like? For

example, what does your heart feel like? Get to know it. Describe that area of your physical body as vividly as you can
- Feel, sense, see the cord. Give it as much description as you can
- Ask what emotion is there. Is there more than one? You may get an answer or simply feel the emotion
- Sit with the emotion. Allow yourself to feel it. You do not need to focus on the cord at this point, simply focus on the emotion
- Visualize, sense, feel the cord. Ask who it goes to
- Repeat the steps of the previous exercise- understand why it is there, what is wants so it can be "cut" or cleared, negotiate or agree to those terms

*Intermediate Emotional Work*

If there is a significant emotion there, you can also take the following steps:
- Feel the emotion. Feel how intense the energy of the emotion is
- How big is that emotion in your body? Is it a specific shape, texture, color? Describe, see, feel the best you can this emotion and where it is in your body
- Now, ask the energy of the emotion to step aside. Frequently, the energy behind an emotion makes it much scarier and bigger than it actually is. We want to talk to, see,

sense the actual emotion, not the energy or momentum behind it. Ask to see the actual emotion (this step gets easier with time)
- Ask the emotion questions
    - what would happen if I were not (angry)?
    - how long have you been there?
    - what age are you from originally?
    - what do you need to clear, change, or shift?
- Listen to the answers. If you can agree to the terms, say so, and then do whatever you agreed to. Negotiate or say no if you are not prepared to do what the emotion is asking

*Some Advanced Emotional Work*

If you have gotten an age (say the anger was from age 4), ask your four-year-old self to come into the room. You would do this by forming a mental image of them. Picture her or him the best you can, and see or sense everything that they are wearing, what they are doing, and how in general they are doing emotionally. See the cord in the same spot in their body as it is in yours. Ask the four year old if they are ready to have the cord removed. If they say yes, remove the cord from both the four year old and you. If they are not, simply revisit it later. This ensures that the cord finally clears and is a big step that people often either do not know about or forget to do.

When we are children often we take on imbalanced cords because we do not know how to appropriately handle energy, or we are in a state of overwhelm due to traumatic or emotional experiences. By going back and envisioning ourselves as the age where the cord is first created, and working with our consciousness at that age to see what we may have needed at that time, the cord will release, and a piece of ourselves that may have been in a state of imbalance can re-integrate with ourselves in a powerful way. By releasing the cord first from the age that it first came about, it is able to clear more easily from our current selves.

This work is very clearing and can create big changes in your life when done. Some of the larger cords may need to be revisited and worked with daily, weekly, or monthly to totally clear. Be patient with this process, and do not force any part of this process. Even if a cord is not ready to clear, just being aware of its presence, or aware of an emotion in your body, is enough to change your life. Even a cord re-balancing or changing to a slightly different state, or releasing some emotions from the cord can allow for significant changes in your life, as well as your relationship to the person who you are corded to. This is difficult and life-changing work, and the strength of people who are willing to release cords like this is admirable.

**Working with Cords with a Lesson Attached**
Often cords remain because there is a lesson for you with a specific relationship that has not been learned yet. This can cause you to continue to be linked to people that you no longer wish to be linked to.

Sometimes, the answer is simply that it takes some time to learn the lessons we are meant to, and divine timing will show us the way. However, there is a simple work-around to this. Divine timing will show us the lesson, but that does not mean that we need the cords there.

When chatting with your cords, simply ask if there is a GENTLE way for you to learn the lesson other than having a cord connected to you. I always stress gentle in my requests because lessons can be difficult and not-so-gentle. Often, this request is granted, and you will learn your lesson another way. You will know that this request is granted when the cord clears or is able to be cut.

You can also try asking for the lesson right there, what you need to know. This sometimes works, but again, divine timing means that you may not be ready for the lesson.

## Clearing Cords of Power and Unequal Relationship

The final cord category is the person on the other end of the cord having power over us. Needless to say, if you feel like someone has done something forced– such as magic– against you to steal your power, you need a competent spiritual practitioner to help you work through that. That can be a part of this category, but mostly cords of power involve parental relationships, teacher/student type relationships, as well as former lovers (and current lovers and partners too), and your way of being in this world.

A cord of power means in basic terms that someone who you are corded to is taking more energy than they are giving. In an ideal relationship, the cord would have an even flow of energy and you would be giving fifty percent, and the person on the other end would be giving fifty percent in order to have this equal and mutually beneficial exchange. This rarely happens, but cords of power would be someone taking energy from you significantly– such as a relationship where they are giving ten percent (or one percent) and you are giving ninety percent (or ninety-nine percent).

A relationship like this is incredibly depleting. We may interact with people such as this and feel exhausted afterwards. Even if we are in a caretaking position, or a position such as therapist, doctor, or holistic therapist we should not be giving away our energy. It is common for people who are out of balance themselves– mentally, physically, or spiritually– to try to cord to people in order to gain energy, sympathy, and power. We can be present with someone, even help someone, without having a cord that is giving away all of our energy, or more than fifty percent of our energy, to another.

An interesting aspect to this dynamic is that once the cords to someone who is stealing power or energy from you are cut or repaired, your relationship is likely to change. It is highly likely that the type of person who is cording and depleting your energy reserves will stop calling you or interacting with you after you do this work. They will have moved on to someone else that they can deplete instead. If you find yourself always the person at social events who dramatic people, or the "energy vampires" of the room converge upon, that will likely change the more you do this work. They simply will gravitate towards others who will allow for them to cord to them and have an imbalanced energetic relationship.

Cords of power can be worked with through conversing with them, like how was done in the other categories. This category is different though in the fact that the reason for this cord remaining is YOU. And solely you- meaning not a relationship. This has to do with your identity, how you are in this world.

What does this mean? In a nutshell, it means that you need to stand up for yourself and take your power back. "Nice" people, empaths, less-dominant personalities, caretakers, healers, gentle souls, and others tend to allow others to dominate and take energy from them. It is wonderful to be a caring soul in this world- to truly give to others from a state of compassion. It is a rare thing, and should be cherished. But this does not mean that you should be filled with toxic cords, or should be giving your personal energy away. When you are able to take a step back, claim your body and your space, and realize that you are worthy of keeping your energy and having equal energetic relationships, this pattern will begin to change. This pattern will continue to change when you regularly work with your cords, clearing and cutting them.

"Energy Vampires"- people who drain others energy to feed energy to themselves, often find and form relationships with people who allow them to do this to them. It is not rare to have partners, friendships, and parental-child relationships revolve around this pattern. One person gives up most of their energy so that the other can take all of the energy. For example, drug addicts are notorious for depleting the energy of family members, and placing toxic cords into people.

*How to Work with Cords of Power*

You can change this pattern with acknowledgement and steady work with it.

- When you notice a cord, ask who it is to and feel or see it in your body. Again, this ability develops over time, and in a short period of time of working with cords regularly it is likely that you will find that you can notice cords easily or through a simple body scan
- Notice if it is draining, adding, or equal energy. Are you giving more than fifty percent of the energy? Are you taking more than fifty percent of the energy?
- If it is draining, you are giving your power away to someone. STOP IT! Relationships should be equal exchanges of energy, even among parent/child and teacher/student and girlfriend/boyfriend

If you notice yourself getting drained, become aware of who is draining you. Say their name out loud. Come up with something to say out loud, like:

*I, (insert name) will no longer allow (Energy Vampire/Unequal Relationship) to take my energy.*

Add more to this statement if you feel the need to. Make it your own, and say it out loud if possible. After you are aware and state this, go on to the next step:

Imagine a cap or seal at the end of your cord to this person. Let the cap or seal cover the cord, and then work with the emotions or needs of the cord to clear it. As long as the cord is there, continue to put a cap or seal over it until the cord is able to be cut or cleared.

    This is such a simple image, but it can have far-reaching results. Patients have repeatedly told me how people stopped draining them, friendships with draining people suddenly stopped, relationships with family members or even the entirety of their family dynamics changed after covering the cord with a cap or seal on a regular basis.

    Often, we allow other people to take our energy because we feel compassion for them. It is difficult to explain to people that it is not right for others to take their energy in any circumstances. If you find yourself being drained of energy by a friend, family member, or partner because they "need" you, or you feel compassion for them because they are upset or acting out, STOP IT!

Beyond that, try this simple trick which will allow for you to see how unequal energetically (and in other ways) this relationship is. It may feel weird at first, but is extremely effective: when someone is draining you, acting out, or you notice yourself feeling compassion or caretaking for someone who is dramatic, emotional or energetically depleting, become aware that you are doing so. You likely feel a little resentful, drained, fatigued, or maybe are taking on their emotions. You don't understand why they are acting this way, because you know it would be so much easier to be or act differently. You now realize through doing cording work that they are likely doing this to take energy from you.

You can stop this with the cap or lid approach, but you can also get a visual of them in your mind. Now ask what their emotional age is. Simple enough. The first time you try this you might feel bad saying that your forty-year-old cousin is emotionally eight years old. When you realize that you are actually speaking to an eight year old in a forty-year-old body, continue to converse with them like they are a forty year old, but realize that they are eight. Would you want an eight year old or allow an eight year old to take energy from you? Would you allow an eight year old to cause you to get angry, tired, or feel their emotions? The answer for most rational people is NO.

The more that you do the "emotional age" exercise, the further reaching and more helpful it is. You can react to the person in traffic differently, your boss, your friends, your family, because you no longer will be energetically reacting to them in the same way. Over time, this person will understand that they cannot get the reaction from you they once did, and more than likely, will stop their behavior, or much more likely, will move on to their next target who they can get a reaction from or drain.

Ultimately, the type of person who allows others to take their energy will have to learn how to stand in their own power and not let other people take advantage of them, but this is an excellent start to learning how to do so.

*What happens now?*
We have gone over several Beginning and Intermediate Methods of how to work with cords. I have taught you the basics of what they are, how to do general as well as specific clearings. I hope you have found this helpful.

Some cord work is helpful to do every day, especially if you are sensitive. I generally suggest doing the basic clearing of your choice when you come home from the day, and doing some of the specific work once or more a week, or whenever you are ready to.

It is common to be impatient, frustrated, or not get answers in the beginning. The more that you do this work, the easier it becomes. The easier it becomes to sense, to see, to feel these cords. So be patient, and continue working with them. Even if you do not sense any cords during your scans, just doing the simple clearings will have profound results.

Both the Basic and Intermediate Cord Work can profoundly change your life and your relationships. People ask me all the time what the effects are of this work, or if the people who the cords are connected to notice anything. The answer is yes, the people who you are connected to will change. Even the most sensitive people will not be able to link it to you working with cords. I have seen time after time the more toxic relationships like "Energy Vampires" simply fall away after this work, and relationships with people you wish to keep (or need to keep) drastically improve. I have also seen relationships, such as marriages, that have a lot of past hurts, be able to turn over a new leaf with this work. Relationships between parent and child that are energetically out of balance have come more into line and become more psychologically healthy with cord work. It may take several cuttings to get to this point, or to garner significant changes in a relationship, but the nature of our connections to people is so important vitally and energetically that this work can and will change your life if you take it seriously.

So what happens after doing this work? Some of these cords that you have cut will reappear. This happens. It is actually a good thing, believe it or not. We want to be connected, to have family, friends, partners, husbands, wives, and neighbors. When these cords are continually cleared they open up the opportunity to start anew with the people in your life, to have a new cord. Continue to cut these cords and let new ones, based on new experiences, new understandings, and the present moment, inform you.

When we continually cut and work with cords the ability to let go of past hurts, traumas, and emotions can help us tremendously in our lives. We can become more whole as individuals, and approach our relationships with less trauma and history of the past.

Something as simple as the cord work here (which really is simple once you get the hang of it, and becomes simpler over time) can have a tremendous impact on your whole life and how you view the world. It truly is one of the easiest and most rewarding forms of energetic and spiritual work that you can do to help yourself.

# Advanced Cord Work

**Introduction**

When we typically talk about a cord, if we do so at all, it is generally thought of as a single cord connecting one human to another. In most basic courses out there a simple cut and clear method is taught and nothing else. This work is of the utmost importance to have clarity in our lives as well as balanced energetic relationships. This subject is unfortunately neglected or not talked about to the depth it deserves by spiritual, occult, and energy work communities. As energy workers we should all have an awareness and understanding about who we are connected to, and what is happening with that connection. Most of all we should be able to discern with certainty what energies are in our bodies, our fields, and the impact that they have on us. All of this can be done with the basic and intermediate work that was detailed in the previous sections.

But in some cases we may wish to have more advanced work for our cording mechanisms. In certain circumstances, for example, we may want to alter cords rather than cut them and start over. We may be more comfortable changing a cord over a period of time because we are not yet ready to fully surrender all of the past traumas or strong emotions that are involved in a particular cord. We also may find that cords are not quite as simple as one cord connecting to us and the other connecting to another living human. When we begin exploring our energetic anatomy and our connections to one another we are likely to find that some of our energy cords look like weavings, or cords to more than one person that may be intertwined.

The further we explore down the energetic rabbit hole we may find ourselves discovering and questioning cords that are not to other humans. We may discover cords that go to other places, spirits, energies, or beings. We may also discover cording mechanisms to past incarnations, to our future self and destiny line, and to our ancestral line, which can bring us great understanding, spiritual revelation, and healing.

When we understand and have direct experience of our energetic anatomy we are also likely to find our energetic blueprint– the grids, lines, and cords that create our energetic, physical, mental, and spiritual structures. Some of these cords, known as natural cords, connect our varying energetic bodies, our midline, and even gives us a direct connection to the cosmos. Each of these is astonishing in scope to realize and work with, and when done properly, the change in both spiritual understanding as well as how you relate to the outer world can undergo massive change.

The advanced work ends with perhaps the most energetically and emotionally significant cording mechanism that we can work with– that of our in-utero connection to our birth mother. Our in-utero experience can be a time of great love, safety, and connection. It can also be a time of panic, worry, fear, drug or anesthetic haze, and the forming of destructive beliefs and understandings about the world and our place in it. By clearing the in-utero cording mechanism we can realize an important connection that we perhaps missed out on, and have our life experience be one of love, safety, and willingness on our part to fully be present in our bodies and here on Earth.

  The intent of each section is to be worked with many times gradually. It is easy when we consider ourselves advanced to want to get exercises, meditations, and spiritual or energetic work accomplished the first time, or quickly. But due to the depth of this work this is rarely a possibility. Each time you decide to work with this section will provide new insight and new depth to your process. For example, once you discover the cord that ties you to the cosmos you will be in awe. But you will also be in awe the seventieth time you work with this cord and discover so much more than the first. So I invite you, with an open mind and heart, to work with these advanced cording mechanisms with the realization that for some of you it may take some time to fully sense and work with these cords. Have patience, and you will persevere.

**How to Alter Cords**

  In the basic and intermediate sections, cords to current relationships were worked with to ensure a fresh start, to release emotions, and to release any sort of stagnant energy or buildup that was present from a cording mechanism that may have been in place for a long time. These cords were released so that they could grow anew based on our current beliefs and understandings about our relationships.

However, in some current relationships we may wish to alter cords rather than completely remove them. If we have a fairly decent relationship with someone and simply want some energetic upkeep, altering the cords can be a perfectly suitable and appropriate way to work with cording mechanisms. On the other hand, if we have a significant and traumatic relationship with someone that we are unable to currently let completely go of, altering the cord bit by bit as we are able to based on our comfort level and readiness to let go may be a preferable way to work.

In either case, altering cords allows for us to focus and reflect on the individual we are corded to, the cord itself between us, as well as the emotions and traumas that may be part of the cord in a more gradual manner. Sitting and really examining a cord and our relationship to someone may be exactly what we need to learn from and understand our relationship. It is likely also true that the more toxic or disruptive the relationship the more difficult it is to release it, or for us to even believe that we once were in such a destructive relationship (or currently are) in the first place. Whatever the case, altering a cord is helpful for those of us who do not wish to simply cut cords but to gradually change, release, and really understand the cord and the relationship to the person we are corded to.

*So How to Alter a Cord?*

The cord between you and another person can be changed, or altered, in many different ways. Some of these ways include: color, texture, thickness, structure, location, composition, and energy. This process is at first the same as the previous course in which we focus on a specific cord, find out whom it is to, and then gain increasing clarity about the cord as we gently focus on it.

As a reminder, finding a cord to work with involves doing a gentle body scan from feet to top of head (not forgetting the arms) asking for an area to highlight where there is a cord. When we find an area that seems stuck, highlighted, or where we may sense or see a cord, we bring our focus to it. We then visualize and feel to the best of our abilities what the cord is like. We then go on to internally describe everything we sense about that cord– color, texture, thickness, and the inner or outer nature of it. By bringing gentle focus to the cord we can then discover emotions that comprise the cord, who is on the other end of the cord, and the energetic nature of the cord.

One of the most common worries people have is about gaining the clarity and knowledge about the cord necessary to fully work with it. For example, people are often very worried if they cannot sense a cord enough to describe it fully, or if they are unable to sense who a cord might go to. Although these worries are understandable, it is through simple focus and gentle exploration that all of these questions, over time, will be answered. So we do not need to strain or force any answers from the cord. We can simply sit with the cord and ask for more clarity, and more information. We can simply ask our bodies innate intelligence to show us a cord and over time it will understand and reveal what we are looking for. By the answers that we are given intuitively from the cord we can discover everything that we want to know about it. It may simply take the discovery of a cord over a period of time to get the answers we are looking for.

So at this point we have discovered a cord we want to work with. This cord is likely to a significant relationship because it did not clear with simple cutting and clearing methods. It likely has unequal energetics (one person is taking more energy than the other), emotions, experiences, and traumas that are stored. This information– our basic history of interacting with the person who the cord goes to– is stored within the cord and colors every experience and interaction we currently have with them. It is difficult to think of the fact that an argument we may have had with someone twenty years ago is still lingering due to an energetic cording mechanism, but it is frequently true. This is one of the reasons why learning how to work with cords is so essential.

So ideally at this point you will have gathered basic information through sitting with a cord– what the cord looks like, who it goes to, and the basic energetics of it.

Now, sit with it until you feel an emotion or two coming up from the cord:

- What is this emotion?
- If you cannot sense an emotion, is there a memory coming up?
- Sit for a few minutes with whatever emotions and memories are coming up. Simply allow for them to be present with you. It is okay if you get upset, or feel emotions. We are doing this so you can bring them to consciousness and release them
- Now, bring your focus back to the cord
- Are you willing to release part of that emotion?
- If the answer is "yes" simply let the cord know that
- If the answer is "no" simply let your focus go back to the cord and sit with it
- If you are willing to release some of the emotion, chances are that the cord has changed visually in some way. Look at the cord and see if any changes have happened
- If you have released some of the emotion, chances are that the felt sense of the cord has changed. Feel how it feels in your body now, and feel the area where it hooks into your body now

Now, we are going to focus on the experiences you may have had with this person. As we all are aware of, even in strong friendships or relationships we occasionally have arguments or difficulties. The energy of this argument may have resolved, but until we release the energetics of the argument at a cord level it may still be a small (or large) part of the unspoken dynamics of our relationship.

In more tumultuous relationships, we may have layers of emotions and experiences that we need to release, and we may need to do so gradually so the experience is not overwhelming. Each section of cord altering can be done multiple times until the look, feel, and sense that the energetics of the cord seem clear and balanced to you.

*Clearing Experiences from the Cord*

It is likely that a memory or two has come up from sitting with the cord. If it has not, ask for a memory from over the course of your relationship to come up. When it does, ask yourself the following questions:

- Do I need to keep this experience energetically with me?
- Do I need to continue holding on to this memory?
- Can I allow this memory to fully come up to clear?
- After you ask yourself these questions, allow for the memory or experience with the person to fully come up. Do not judge it, and attempt to observe it with compassion
- When you are ready, ask yourself if you would rather keep this cord how it is with its charged emotions and experiences or to let some, or all of it go

A few words about the experience of letting something go. When you do so it is not like you will not remember the person, or will forget the experience. But when something is triggered, such as a memory that had heightened emotions or a less than pleasurable experience, there is a part of us that is continuously subconsciously and repeatedly experiencing this until we are able to resolve it. So the basic question is not if we never want to remember this person or the experience again (although this may be exactly what you want, depending), but if you want to allow yourself to continue to be experiencing on a sort of loop the memory that is coming up for you.

When you are ready, you will let the cord know directly if you are ready to let the memory, the emotions, or whatever else is coming up, fully or partially go. It is okay if you say "no", and it is okay if you are only able to partially let go. Even the experience of recalling the memory will allow for a portion of it to resolve.

After you tell the cord this, again check in with the cord and see if it has visually changed, or if the felt sense of it has changed. If it has not, that is fine, but chances are that it has in some way. The above (releasing emotions and memories) can be done multiple times, but when the cord seems less charged (meaning you are not getting strong memories or emotions from it) working with the core energetics of it is helpful.

*Altering the Energetics of the Cord*

This time when you bring gentle focus back to the cord you are going to focus on the energetic nature of it. If you are naturally sensitive, this may be easy for you. If you are not, or are having some difficulty, focus on the visual or felt sense of the cord to whatever extent it remains and ask the following questions:

- If I could feel or sense the cord, what would I see or feel?
- Ask the cord to heighten its energy. What do you sense about the energetics of the cord?
- Remember, the cord is intended to have even, reciprocal flow between you and the person you are corded to
- Does your cord have even flow both giving and receiving of energy?
- If it does not, what percentage are you giving of energy? 10? 60 percent?
- If it does not, what percentage are you receiving of energy from the other person? 10 percent? 80 percent?

Once you have a basic understanding of cord energetics (how much energy you are giving and receiving) you may want to change these dynamics. Again, ideally in all of our relationships we would be giving and receiving fifty percent, meaning equally. This is rarely the case, however, and the more out of balance we are, the more out of balance our relationship likely is.

Although gone over in the previous course, there are many of us walking around with extremely out of balance energetic cords. We may be corded to someone who is taking 90 percent of the energy of our relationship. We may feel fatigued, upset, or just simply drained without knowing why due to an extremely imbalanced cord, or have many cords that are just slightly out of balance that are creating issues for us.

While doing these exercises it is normal to feel a sense of guilt come up with releasing out of balance relationships. If we have found ourselves taking a bunch of energy from someone we may feel guilty for dominating our relationship energetically. If we find ourselves giving all, or most of our energy away, we may realize on some level that we are doing so. Even so, when confronted with the cord and the energetic dynamics of the relationship, we may balk at changing anything. This is because we may be used to giving all of our energy away to loved ones. If we have a dominating child, lover, or dramatic friend we may feel like we *have to* on some level give them our energy so they can function.

Although this dynamic is understandable, neither the giver nor receiver of energy is in a good, whole, and balanced state if the energetics of the cord are at 90/10, or even 30/70. We can love and support someone without giving them our vital energy. If you find yourself not wanting to release a cord that is detrimental, or significantly out of balance, ask yourself the following questions:

- What do you fear would happen if the cord were more balanced?
- Is that fear something you are willing to release, or release part of?
- If yes, let the cord know that
- If no, or you find yourself resisting or finding excuses to not release, allow yourself to simply sit with the understanding that you are resisting
- Can you allow yourself to feel that resistance?
- Completely immerse yourself in that resistance. Allow for it to fully come up so you can experience it
- Accept that you are resistant and give yourself permission to fully feel that resistance
- Allow for that resistance to surround you like a bubble
- When you are ready, visualize yourself popping that bubble
- Take a breath, and go back to the emotions or memory release, and then evaluate the energetics of the cord again

*Re-working the Energetic Balance of the Cord*

Now that you have evaluated the energetics of the cord, you are ready to change them.

Imagine the cord like it were a straw with energy flowing through it from you to the other person:

- What colors would that energy be?
- Would the flow be thick, thin, fast, slow?
- Visualize or sense the dynamics you discovered before– of energy flowing from you to the other person, and from the other person to you
- Allow yourself to let go of any emotions or experiences coming up
- Now, if this cord were to flow differently and in a more balanced way, how would that flow be?
- Ask the cord if it would be willing to do so
- Now, ask the outer components of the cord (the actual straw part) if it were to be a different color, texture, or thickness, how would it be?
- Ask the cord if it is willing to do so
- Re-evaluate the cord, sensing the energetic dynamics. Has it improved? How would you evaluate it in terms of percentage now?
- Go back and repeat this portion until the cord is willing to change. It should have a clear, equal flow with a pleasant color. There should be no grime, dirt, or muck inside of the cord. There should be a sense of lightness in the area where the cord is attached or anchored in to your physical body

*Working with the Anchor*

In terms of energetic anatomy, each cord has an energetic line, or straw-like mechanism that goes between us and another person. Each cord also has a hook, or anchor-like mechanism that grounds the cord into our energetic and physical bodies. It is typical for people with toxic cords (very imbalanced and heavily laden with emotion and trauma) to have pain in their physical bodies where the cord attaches and anchors in to the physical body. However, sensitives and psychics may be especially aware of cords and cording mechanisms and may feel pulling sensations, heaviness, or simply something present in areas where large or small cords are present.

As we have gone over in the previous course, most cords anchor into the chakra system, particularly in the torso. It is possible to have a cord anchor anywhere in the body, but the chakra system has a lot of vital energy so there is a tendency for cords to hook into those areas. It is also more likely for significant cords to attach near or on the midline of the body, simply because of the depth of those relationships, while less significant or random cords that are more easily cleared or cut can and will hook into the physical body pretty much anywhere and will have less significant anchors, if they have one at all.

So since we have worked with the cording mechanism the next thing to do is to work with the anchor. This can be done by another simple questioning process. It is also of note that where the anchor is placed in our bodies currently may not be the appropriate place for it. It is possible to change where the cord is hooked in to our physical bodies to make it more appropriate for energetic exchange, as well as more comfortable overall.

First, you will simply again sit with the cord you are working on and visualize, sense, or feel it the best that you are able to at this moment:

- Now, you will focus on where the cord attaches into your physical body. This may be a straight line in or may curve into the body from the cord itself
- Once you get a sense of where the cord attaches into the physical body, you will ask for the felt sense of the anchor, or place the cord is attached, to heighten
- Sit with this for a few minutes, noting any details that come up, including emotions, pains, felt sense, and visuals
- Now, focus gently on the attachment area and anchoring mechanism
- What does this anchor look like? What shape is it?
- What does the anchor feel like? Is it causing any distress in your physical body to have it there?
- How deep is it in the body? Some cords attach in the energy body (they do not attach to the physical body). Others may attach to just under the skin layer, or to organs, muscle, or to the spine. It is okay if you do not know the name of the

- organ or muscle if you feel it attached to one. Just get a sense of how deep the anchor is in your body
- When you discover all of this information, does it seem like the anchor is in balance? By this I mean that it is in the right spot, that it is at the appropriate depth, and that it is the appropriate size, color, texture, and is not creating uncomfortable sensations in your body
- If it does seem in balance, you can just sit with the cord and go back to the previous sections, making sure that the energy flow and the cord itself are feeling in balance as well
- If it does not seem in balance, you will at first simply ask the anchor and attachment into the physical body and ask it to come to a state of balance
- Ask for the cord to release any emotions or energy that is needed for it to come to a state of balance

It is likely that the cord has changed or shifted in some way. You can simply go back and ask for it to come to a state of balance again and again with simple awareness.

If you feel as if something is resistant, or unresolved, you may want to sit with the anchor and attachment mechanism and again question what it needs to release.

- Directly ask the anchor what it needs to release or come to a more balanced state
- Get a sense of the answer. Again, this may be an intuitive sense or reply. Trust your intuition with the answers you are receiving. If the answer isn't quite right you can always go back and do this exercise again later, or change the answer when you come upon the right one
- Internally ask (this is more general, to your basic intuition and not to the cord) what is preventing you from releasing this anchor
- What would happen if you did release this anchor, or allowed for it to come into a state of balance?
- If emotions come up, simply allow for them to do so. It is okay to feel grief, pain, anger, and/or fear
- What would happen to your relationship with the person on the other end of the cord if you released this anchor, or allowed for it to be in balance?

A common thought here is that the person on the other end of the cord has some sort of power or control over you, which is creating a lack of change, or resistance to change. In terms of energetic anatomy, this is only true on their end– for their anchor. The most common reason that the anchor on our end is not willing to re-balance is because of our own emotions and fears about our relationship with the person in question. We may be unable to forgive them for something they have done, want to control them or their behavior, or are holding on because we still long for acceptance from them. It is only by taking personal responsibility for our selves, physically and emotionally, that we can allow for ourselves to come into a state of balance. This simply means that at some point if you are sitting with an anchor to a cord that still feels painful, emotional, or out of balance, that we must question our own energy in the relationship:

- Do we want to have control over the person?
- Do we want acceptance from them on some level?
- What would happen to our own lives if we released this anchor to them?
- Can we forgive this person for what they might have done to us?
- Do we want to hold on to the emotions, the pain, control, the seeking of acceptance… or do we want to be in balance, healthier, and clearer?

If we sit with these questions for a bit, we may realize that we can simply release the charged emotions, experiences, and ideas that we have created that are causing an imbalanced cord. By coming to the appropriate realizations through sitting with these questions, we can again ask the anchor if it is willing to rebalance. As we are able to let go of the layers of control, acceptance, or forgiveness we may need from the person by doing this exercise several times, the anchor will naturally release and come to a balanced state. If the anchor does seem like it needs some help, the visualization of the sun going through your body from the beginning section of this book should help to release any remaining residual energies and emotions that need to clear.

*Re-Placing Cords*

Through working with cords we may come to the realization that the cord simply is attached in the wrong place. As we come to a more accepting nature of a situation or person we may realize that the cord, which was originally located in our Liver area (under the ribcage to the right, for example) would be healthier if it was in our solar plexus area. We may be in a highly sexual, charged relationship with a cord attached to our genitals and first chakra, and realize that we want more depth out of the relationship and that the cord would ideally be in the heart area.

All cords should ideally be anchored into the midline of our body. It is natural for cords to less important relationships, such as the interaction we had with a random person in the grocery store, to have a faint cord from really anywhere in the body. But ideally cords to any relationships that we wish to keep (as in not clear, cut, and remove) will be located midline in our torso. Cords that attach too far up, such as to the throat, third eye, and crown, tend to be imbalanced and based in illusion and fantasy. Cords that attach to the first chakra and genitals tend to be highly charged, sexual, or filled with emotions and drama.

In an ideal state, cords would be attached to the second through fourth chakra (lower abdomen to heart or high heart, just under where the clavicles meet), would have minimal anchoring with no pulling or discomfort when focused on, and a balanced, even flow of energy. As has been discussed, that is rarely the case. The closer that we can come to this ideal cord is the clearer and more balanced our relationships as well as our energy field will be.

Even with this being said, it is important for the cord you are working with to come to a balanced state for you. This means that although the concept of an ideal cord has been discussed, if a cord you are working with feels at home slightly off midline, and seems balanced emerging out of the throat, that is of the highest importance. So trust your intuition, that internal sense of guidance, and allow for the cord to come to a balanced state that is perfect for you.

The last aspect of working with simple cords to another human being is to re-place, or rather re-home them. This may happen naturally as we come to a more balanced state through the questioning process and the release of layers of emotions and experiences. But frequently the cord itself may change, the anchor may change, and it still is in the same place, even if it is not the correct place. This is due to the angle and trajectory of the cord, as well as that it seems that for whatever reason the cord doesn't naturally understand that part of the balancing process may be relocating to a more suitable place.

We may choose to dissolve cords and anchors through sunlight, as was taught in the previous course. We may also choose to move the cords ourselves, or help them to realize that they are not in the correct place:

- Sit with the anchor of the cord with gentle focus
- You may have already realized that the cord is not in the correct place, or you may wish to question if the cord should be in another location
- At first, you will simply ask the cord if it is willing to move to a more suitable location
- If so, ask where. Chances are that it will want to move to the nearest chakra
- Gently guide it to the nearest chakra by cupping your hand and imagining it going into your body to the depth of the anchor
- You will then slide the anchor with the accompanying cord to the location it wants to move to
- When it does move, sit with the cord for a moment and ensure that it feels that it is in the correct location
- If it feels correct, sit with the cord, anchor, and the energy flow of the cord for a few moments to ensure that it feels complete.
- If it does not feel correct after it has moved, gently sit with the cord and ask for your body to highlight or in some way show you where the cord should be

- When this area is highlighted, you will again gently cup your hand and slide the anchor up to the appropriate location
- If the cord does not want to move, or is resistant to moving fully into a new location, go back and work with the cord itself as well as the anchor to clear emotions and energy

It may take multiple times of working with a cord so that it feels comfortable enough to be in its correct location. When a cord is in its correct location and it has been cleared of unhealthy or imbalanced emotions and energies it should stop having resonance. This means that once a cord is healthy it simply will not show up as something for you to work with, and will no longer be something that you notice physically, mentally, or even energetically. The most energetically sensitive of us will notice cords, but a cord that is in balance and in its correct location will simply be something that we notice– not something that creates any sort of physical discomfort, will not be emotionally charged in a negative manner, and will not highlight when we ask for a cord to work with through these exercises.

In a balanced state, we will simply notice a clean, brightly colored cord or simply energy or electricity going from us to another person that has equal energetic flow in and out.

It is important to do cord work frequently. Even if we have achieved the "ideal" cord, it is likely that due to our complex, messy relationships and the many events that happen interpersonally in our lives that we need to perform upkeep on even the most balanced of cords. The good news is that doing upkeep is typically much easier than lifting off the initial layers of energies of a cord.

The more that we do this work the more we can have balanced relationships and a clear energetic field. The ability to have a clear energetic field is essential for any sensitive, spiritual worker, or really anyone who works with the public at any level (especially in healthcare and positions of service) to ensure that we are full of vital energy, are able to release anything that is not ours, and so we can ensure that we are not being drained or de-vitalized by any relationship that we may have.

The ability to do cord work at this an advanced level truly allows for us to have clarity and balance in our relationships, as well as to heal past hurts and traumas on a deep level. We can do all of the therapy, all of the emotional and spiritual healing work that we can find– but until we are able to work with the energetic blueprint of our relationship (the cord and anchor) we are likely to find ourselves not able to fully release past hurts and emotions, not able to move on from relationships that have ended, and not able to have the sort of love and balanced energy we would like from the people we have in our lives.

*Thoughts on Cording and Shielding*
One of the most common things that people do in energy work is to erect shielding or protection mechanisms. These do work to a

certain extent, some more successfully than others. In an emergency situation, such as having to have lunch with an especially toxic colleague or have to interact with an energy vampire family member at a function, we may find it necessary to imagine shields, glass, or really anything to have that person not have an effect on us, or such a large effect on us.

But outside of emergency situations the tendency to shield and protect can cause us great detriment. Ideally our energy body (or bodies) will be flowing fully– both in and out, and we will be in a state of feeling the tides of the cosmos, our environments, and one another. Our ability as human beings striving to become more conscious should be to become more clear and less chaotic. Adding on mechanisms, such as shields, that interfere with the clarity of our energy fields, and the natural influx and outpouring of energies should be something that is carefully considered before doing. We also have a tendency to use our own vital energy when blocking others, which means that we can easily become fatigued through our efforts to protect ourselves.

By instead resolving any negative emotions, healing past traumas, and clearing our energy field we can become healthier, more balanced individuals who are able to deeply immerse ourselves in larger flows of energy. By releasing, instead of constricting or protecting, we can find ourselves happy, healthy, and more balanced individuals.

## Tangled and Woven Cords

In some cases, cords can be tangled or woven. This occurs either because more than one cord has tangled together, or because an outside energy has attached to the cord for energy or sustenance. It is much more common for a cord to be tangled to more than one person, however, than for us to even notice that an outside energy has latched to the cord.

Tangled and woven cords typically occur because we are linked to people who share a similar history, experiences, or timeline. For example, it is likely that due to the nature of our relationships to our family that cords going out to both of our siblings may become tangled due to our close relationship and shared history. We may also have two interwoven cords going to our roommates from college, or have one large cord that has woven into it all of our romantic relationships. A client who was in a bus crash had cords to all of the survivors woven together, and a particularly high-level Empath (very sensitive person who tends to take on energy through absorption and reflection) had one large cord with multiple woven strings surrounding it to all of the people who she met and absorbed energy from over a twenty year period. Each new person she would meet would add another string onto the larger cord.

There are other situations than those above where we might have tangled, woven, or intermingling cords. In this case, and similar cases, either a mass of cords will appear that have strings or a similar image binding them together, or we are unable to have clarity with a particularly thick cord that we may find. This might present as you being unable to tell who a cord goes to because several people pop into your head during the questioning process, and upon further examination the cord doesn't seem to be straightforward– it is curved, tangled, or in some way doesn't appear like the other cords in your system. If you are more of a felt sense person, this cord may feel simply "off" to you or you may realize when working with the cord that it has a more complex quality to it.

This pattern is somewhat rare, meaning that it should not be the first thing that you look for or expect, but it is common enough that most people interested in the advanced aspects of energy work should know how to work with it.

To work with this section you should have already gone through the basic, intermediate, and advanced course work in the previous sections. This will allow for you to fully see or sense that you have a cord that is tangled, or multiple cords that are tangled together, and for you to work with some of the basic emotional, spiritual, and energetic causes for cords.

It can be difficult to figure out who exactly cords are to if they are woven or tangled together. To do this work it is not important to fully understand this, although our conscious mind of course always wants to know. Once the cords are cleared and separated the realization of who they are to will appear. When you have found a tangled or woven cord you will sit with it and fully acknowledge what you are seeing or sensing. This may at first be that this cord has multiple layers and levels of cording or that it creates sensations that are unlike any other cords you have worked with. You may also completely lack any sort of clarity about whom a cord goes to. Instead of getting frustrated allow yourself to sit with the confusion and realize that the cord may simply be more complex, multi-layered, or woven together in such a way that it would be difficult to have clarity with it.

It should be noted that if it is revealed that the cord goes to anything other than a living human (such as a deceased human, a spirit, a place, or is a cord that seems like a natural part of your energetic anatomy) that these will be covered in upcoming sections of this book. But for now we will work with any cords that appear tangled or woven:

- First, you will sit with the woven or tangled cord. Get the best visual or felt sense of the cord that you can
- Now, as if you were talking directly to the cord (or cords) you will ask if the cord(s) are woven or tangled by an inner (meaning due to your own) or outer (meaning an outside force) binding
- If it is by an outside force, meaning that it does not have to do with you or the people on the other end of the cord you will move on to the next section
- If it is tangled or woven due to you or inner forces, you will continue by simply acknowledging that information

- Ask for the information about the cord to heighten. Allow for sensations, visuals, and felt sense to focus and heighten of the cording mechanism, its tangles, or its looped or woven nature

Once you have a good sense of how the cord looks and feels you are welcome to draw it, which for some sensitives can allow for them to fully "see" the cord in a way they were not able to through vision, or to simply continue.

In this work I choose to work with the energy of Spider medicine to unravel, reweave, or untangle cords, but this may not be the correct choice for you. There are plenty of weavers throughout history, such as the Moirae, Holda, Arachne, Athena, the Norns, and others who might be useful for this function. If you are doing this work, you should be familiar with how to approach and ask a spirit, deity, or being for permission to call them forward to assist you. If not, looking up basic journey techniques with the intent of finding a spiritual helper who can work with weaving that is right for you will be of help.

Otherwise, I would suggest looking to the mythology of your own culture to see who the weavers are and to journey to them to ask if they are willing to assist you.

Since Spider is traditional and appears in many cultures, I will be utilizing her here for this work. But as with any spiritual work, it is important to form relationships with the energies that are appropriate and work well for you.

*Reweaving and Detangling with Spider*

At this point you should have a good visual or felt sense of the tangled, woven, or otherwise difficult cord or cords. You are welcome to utilize the following words below, or feel free to create your own, suitable for the energy you are working with or that have personal resonance and power for you.

*I call in Grandmother Spider to untangle these cords. Let her clear and release any cords that are tangled, let her reweave that which is broken, unmanageable, looped, or otherwise is unclear. I give my thanks for any releasing and reweaving, and offer immense gratitude for her ability to clear and release any emotions, traumas, or other energetic or spiritual forces that are causing these cords to be tangled, unclear, or stuck together. Please allow these cords to become clear so I may further work with them.*

At this point Spider should naturally come through and begin detangling and reweaving the cords. If you are not a visual person it is likely that your felt sense of the cord with change. It is always appropriate with any spirit that comes through to express gratitude for their work. The words above are a simple calling in of Spider and asking for cords to be returned to a somewhat balanced state- it is perfectly appropriate to change the wording to suit your particular situation. For example, if you find that a cord is broken, or stuck together, you may wish to ask specifically for that to be resolved. If there are several cords tangled together, you may wish to ask for separation of the cords. If you lack clarity on who the cords go to, or are unable to fully see or sense the cords, you can make clarity the primary focus of what you say to Spider.

The purpose of reweaving the cord after it has been untangled or cleared is so that the cord can become more balanced. We are intended to have cords to the people in our lives, but the ideal cord will be one separate cord to each person in our lives. Spider is ideal for reweaving, reconnecting, and separating cords so that we can come closer to that ideal. After we work with Spider we may find that we need to go back and do individual basic, intermediate, or advanced cord work on the newly separated, untangled cord in order to achieve the balance we would like in that particular cord.

If a cord is particularly knotted, curved, or there are many cords woven together you may find it beneficial to at first visit an experienced energy worker or spiritual healer who is knowledgeable about cords. Sometimes we need an outside catalyst, such as a spiritual worker or energy worker, to help us get through particularly difficult cording mechanisms. This is especially true if we try to work with our cords and find ourselves frustrated because not much is happening, or we feel resistance or blockage in doing so. Since cords like this contain so much energy, and typically from many different sources, it is well worth our while to go visit an outside healer, or to have patience while we connect with Spider multiple times in order to work with a complex pattern such as this.

*Outside Energetic Interference*

It is much more typical in the case of woven or tangled cords to have it be an issue of multiple cords tied together, or complex emotions or other entanglements creating an energetic weaving or knotting with our cording mechanisms. It is also much more typical for us, as human beings, to notice our woven and tangled human-based cords rather than ones that have spiritual influences creating imbalances. However, there can be an outside energy or force interfering or latching on to the cording mechanism. This will create a sort of darkness or energy that surrounds the cord, or a pressure that comes from the outside of the cord going in.

This may, at first, appear similarly to the tangled or woven nature of the previous patterns. Upon inquiry we may find that the knots, tangles, or energies surrounding the cord are caused by a spiritual or energetic interference. We may in fact be able to see or sense a source of congestion, darkness, dinginess, cloudiness, or something tangled surrounding the cord that comes from an outer source.

What can tangle a cord or create this type of darkness could fill an entire book. Astral energies, which are lower-level energetic beings, are very likely, as are many other spirits, energies, and beings, both conscious and non-conscious. Simple human jealousy from an outside source, if strong enough, can cause this to happen in relationship cording mechanisms. We live in a sea of energy in which most of us can only see or sense a small spectrum. When we begin doing work like this we are likely to begin "waking up" to more of the spectrum of consciousness. In doing so we will increase our ability to see or sense the sheer amount of spiritual stimuli that surrounds us.

While there are many benevolent, kind spirits and energies (or at the very least energies that do not really care about us so as not to interfere with us, our energy, or our lives) there are also energies that will interfere with cords. These energies are more likely to interfere with cords that are either really toxic and imbalanced, or the cords that have an incredibly high amount of flowing energy through them. Both types are not attaching to cords antagonistically– they are most likely looking to feed off of the toxic or negative thoughts and emotions… or of the pure heart-centered emotions that higher vibration cords can involve.

In the case of energies attracted to "lower" cords, such as cords that have a history of trauma, lots of emotions, and a rather toxic nature, it is natural for these energies to simply release from the cord once we do our personal work with such a cord– releasing trauma, charged emotions, and correcting any significant energetic imbalances in energy flow. Quite simply, some energies are looking to feed on toxic energy. If we no longer have toxic energy or interactions, the energies feeding off of the cord will simply lift off and go elsewhere.

It is often the case that a highly sensitive, psychic, or spiritually aware sort of person to have all sorts of energies wanting assistance, simply surrounding the person with interest, or looking to feed off of the energy that the person gives off. In previous works I have compared the spiritually aware or "awake" person to a nightlight. The more we are able to sense or see and/or the more aware we are the brighter our nightlight is. When we are able to see or sense so much we are not only able to see and sense a broader spectrum of energy but we can be seen as well. Most people have a pretty dim nightlight (if theirs is burning at all) so if someone has a nightlight that is casting a huge amount of light into the darkness (darkness being a metaphor for the spirit world, essentially) the more spirits and other energies are going to notice.

This means that people who are sensitive or more aware are the most likely to have things like spirit attachments, or to have energies of all sorts look to swarm the proverbial nightlight like moths. This also means that our energy body can become clouded, and energies can look to feed off of the energy we give off, especially in our cording mechanisms.

The good news about this is that we can set the intent that any energy that is attached to us or in our field will transform instead of being fed. It is a huge problem for natural energy workers and sensitives to have a variety of energies attached to them or in their field without their recognizing it. This is partially because many energy workers, spiritual workers, and sensitives lack the basic skills and tools to know how to release such energies and to properly cleanse, but is also because it is natural for us to consciously (or unconsciously) be working with the energetic and spiritual realms throughout our days which means that we will naturally collect these types of energies.

As was mentioned, to work with any energy that is latched on due to toxic emotions the individual cord work is essential to do first. This means releasing emotions, traumas, and possibly re-homing the cord, as well as making sure that there is proper energetic flow through the cord. It is only then that energies that are feeding off of the emotions will naturally, or through this exercise, release.

If you are a naturally awake or sensitive person there is no work that needs to be done prior to doing the following exercise. It is definitely much easier for sensitives and awakened individuals to complete the following work, but will also need to be done more often by that population as well:

- First, you will acknowledge that you are constantly with source energy (meaning cosmic, divine, and so forth energy)
- Now, sit with your midline (your spine) and heart. Just allow yourself to feel the energy that runs through the midline of your body. This should feel like a stream or flow or water
- From the midline of your body imagine a door opening. This is the door to full source energy
- This will reveal a column of light emanating from you. You can fully open the door to fully release this energy, or open the door slightly to simply have the column pour out

- Allow for this light to flow through you and into your energetic field. It should surround you approximately six inches away from your physical body, if not more
- Ask for this energy to heal and release anything that is not yours
- Ask for this energy to heal and release anything attached to your energetic cords
- We may choose, after this work, to simply close the door. We are likely to find that it also closes naturally

This meditation can be done until we realize that we fully are source. When we come to this understanding we can simply emanate this light, focused on the specific energy looking to feed off of our cords, and it will be healed and released. Until then we will need to imagine the doorway opening so that we are able fully emanate the amount of light we require to clear such energies.

    It is typical when first starting (or even at advanced stages) to have an adversarial relationship to the spirit world. Anything that is causing us harm, or even anything we notice, we want to automatically clear or destroy. When we are able to become fully aware we will realize that spirits and beings that attach to cords like this are simply looking for energy. We can treat them with compassion and offer them healing and release. It should be said that even with compassion comes boundaries. This means that there should be nothing in our bodies or our energetic field that is not vitally us, and that does not have our permission to be there.

If we are having particular difficulties with energies that look to attach to us or our cords we may want to visit an energy worker or spiritual worker focused on Rootwork, or Spiritual Herbalism. The practice of spiritual bathing with a prescribed regimen of herbs by a knowledgeable healer can be essential for sensitives to not only clear energies like this, but to maintain overall health, vitality, and boundaries.

**Cording to Places and Events**
Through careful examination of our cords to people we are likely to feel more energized, more aware, and to develop better health and vitality. Through clearing and working through the beginning, intermediate, and advanced work we may also begin to notice cords that are not to other living people. If we are ready for advanced energetic work that is rarely noticed or taught (and goes way below the surface knowledge of most teachers, students, and seekers) we may even begin to notice cords that are natural extensions of our energetic anatomy.

But once we work through the previous work it is more likely at first to become increasingly aware that we have cords to non-living people, such as to spirits, energies, beings, and even to places and events. Like cording to people, it is entirely natural and appropriate to cord to places, or to have a cord to an event that was a crucial part of our own spiritual evolution. But similar to our cords to people, these cords to places and events can become toxic, clogged, or simply stop us from moving forward in our lives.

The most common symptom of this is an obsession with a specific place or event. These are the people who cannot stop talking about how they were a cheerleader in high school, or who wish they were still seventeen years old. This is the person who went on a vacation to Mexico five years ago and still cannot stop talking about it. We also can be obsessed with a rock concert, a social event or party, or really anything that we engaged in at one time of our lives and found significant. We may find ourselves similarly obsessing about a place we have not visited but is part of our cultural heritage, an event that we always wanted to attend but have not had the chance to yet, or a school that we wish we could attend.

It is entirely natural and appropriate to be excited about the events in our lives and the places we have visited. It is even balanced to think about places that we feel a call to visit, or events or schools we dream about attending. What happens in many of these situations, however, is that the cording mechanism to this place is not allowing for us to move on from this vacation or concert, this event or place. There is a part of us energetically that is not only focused on this part of our past but is stagnated in it. When this happens we are not fully present, and our energy is not all accounted for. This means that we cannot fully be energized, complete, or happy because we are corded to a separate aspect of ourselves who is not part of our current consciousness and present-day reality, such as our seventeen-year-old self who is still playing guitar in his high school band.

As a point of clarity, there are some energy workers and spiritual workers who take "clearing" too literally. There is an idea that you must completely clear, or not think about, really anything but the present moment. This idea continually brings forward new literature about "changing" or "clearing" any stories that you have, or visualizing new ones instead of the ones that were possibly chaotic or traumatic. While the mental aspects of this type of work can be effective on a surface level, we do not need to completely forget about our vacation to Ireland, or not think about how much fun we had in our twenties. When we focus on clearing the energetics and spiritual nature of things (rather than the mental) we naturally stop being obsessive, and we naturally become more whole, present human beings.

We can still think about that wonderful vacation we had last year, or how we want to visit New Zealand. It is the imbalanced state and the cording mechanism that is splitting our energy that needs to be resolved so that we can become whole– and the memories or wishes of places or events can simply be thoughts rather than obsessions or things that divide our consciousness.

When we do the following work we can call back all of the pieces of ourselves that have split off or are engaged elsewhere. By calling these cords back and resolving them we can become more present, more whole, and actually have enough energy to go off and do the things we want to do and visit the places we want to visit. When we are engaged in cording to places or events we can never fully realize who we are as people– because some of our energy is actually still present in the time, place, and event that we are corded to. By reclaiming our cords to places and events we can move forward in our destiny and on our path with full power and clarity.

*How to Recall Cords to Places and Events*
Similar to working with cords to people, we are going to do a general cord clearing or recall. Later, we are going to work with the cords that remain to significant places and events.

- First, you are going to get a general sense of cords that may be to places or events. If you have worked through the prior material, these cords should be fairly clear
- If you are unable to sense cords to different places or events you can still continue with this work. Ideally, you will in some way sense, ask for, call up into consciousness, draw, or enter a meditative state where you can sense them
- You will begin by simply asking these cords to return to you. Imagine them returning to you like reeling in a fishing line
- Ask for all the parts that are separate from you, in another place, time, or still participating in a past event to return to you

Although this seems simple, this general "reeling in" of cords to places and events can be extremely effective. Such reeling in is especially helpful for all different types of situations where we might want to return "home" to our bodies- such as traveling on an airplane, after a stressful period of life where we might disassociate due to trauma, or even due to a hangover.

When we generally become aware that such cords exist and ask for them to return to us they should naturally resolve energetically within our system as long as we reel them in to our physical body. If things still feel unresolved you can move on to the next part where we will be working with significant cords to places and events, or you may choose to work with source energy through the doorway method taught in the last section to dissolve any remaining residual energy from the general cord recall that was just done.

It is more than likely that some of our cords to places and events did not resolve through the general cord recall. This is because these places and events are significant- in this case meaning that we have a significant portion of ourselves energetically elsewhere. These cording mechanisms need to be worked with on an individualized basis to resolve.

*Individualized Resolving of Cords to Places or Events*
With significant portions of ourselves energetically elsewhere it is important to find resolution with the aspect of Self that still remains at a certain place or with an event that has happened. Through this process we can individually gather aspects of ourselves that are corded elsewhere, resolve past incomplete

events, and fully become embodied and present in our physical body.

In other spiritual work, the process of Soul Retrieval can be strikingly similar and can in fact be substituted some of the time. The main difference is a focus on place, as well as a focus on any aspect of Self that is stagnated– not just the traumatized aspects that the Soul Retrieval process tends to focus on. In further work, such as the section of *Cording to the Future Self and Destiny Line* we can realize our destiny, and take the energy that has been misused or simply elsewhere to propel ourselves forward into the path or destiny that we are meant to be following with the entirety of our being.

Although seemingly complex in terms of number of steps, the process of resolving cords to individual places and events is somewhat simple. First, you are going to think about or ask for a place or event that you are corded to. This can be done by sitting in a meditative state and asking for one to appear, or simply thinking logically about a place, event, or aspect of self (like you at seventeen, or thirty, or fifty-five) that you still think regularly about or even obsess about. You will then go through a basic journey or meditation to find this aspect of Self, ask what it needs to resolve, and clear it. After this a basic cord cutting, clearing, or the source doorway method will resolve the remaining cord.

This process is written out so you can follow along step by step:

- Think about a place, event, or age that you simply cannot get off your mind. You either think about this often, or may even obsess about it
- What age were you?
- Now, visualize yourself at the place or event if you have been there. If you have not, skip to the next section
- Describe the scene and your self the most vividly that you can– what are you wearing? What is going on? What emotions are you feeling?
- Let yourself feel fully immersed in this place or event
- Now, imagine a cord extending from that self to your current self
- Describe the cord as vividly as you can
- Switch your attention back to you at this event or place. Let yourself know that you can have the memories and feelings from this place, but that it is not balanced to have an aspect of yourself out of body or still engaged energetically with this place or event
- Ask this version of you if it is willing to return so that you can become fully embodied
- If not, ask what it would need to feel okay returning. Again, state that you will still have the memories, experiences, and feelings from this place

- Work with this version of Self until you can provide it what it needs. This may be several things, or just one. You do this by simply asking what they need, and visualizing this occurring for this version of you, and then asking again if they would be okay with returning
- When they are willing to return, you will gently have them walk towards you, picking up the slack in the cord
- They will simply walk into you with the cord and begin to integrate
- You will then do the source doorway method or imagine sunlight running through you to fully integrate

This method is effective at getting back pieces of you still engaged in an event or place visited. The question always arises about what harm it can do if we are otherwise engaged– meaning that if there is an aspect of ourselves energetically still a football captain, or leader of the debate team, a wild twenty or thirty-something, or at our favorite place– why we cannot simply be there. The answer to this is that to be fully, vitally who we are in a current lives we need to be embodied. We need to be responsible for our energy, and having energetic portions of ourselves elsewhere leads to feeling scattered and the ability to not really fully participate in our current lives. The more that we are fully, energetically here, the more that we will be able to feel whole, secure with who we are, and have the sort of energy and vitality to pursue our dreams and passions in our current day and current selves.

The prior method is excellent for returning those aspects of Self that are otherwise engaged with past events or places visited. However, we may find ourselves obsessed with places we have never visited or events that we have never attended. This may be for a variety of reasons– from simple wishful thinking to the influence of past lives or ancestral sources. Whatever the reason, if we find ourselves obsessed with a place or a strong desire to simply be elsewhere, it is important to pull our energy back into our selves. This is for the same reason as the previous section– we cannot fully and vibrantly be a part of our current daily lives if we are elsewhere. We may also find, oddly, that when we do this work that we actually have the opportunity to visit these places or take part in the activities or events we have been obsessing over. It is by letting go of the obsession and returning to ourselves fully that we can actually take charge and make the changes (and plans) from a balanced, whole state that will allow for us to fully move forward as we should in our lives.

- Similar to the last method, you will visualize the place or event that you have been dreaming about or obsessed with
- Even if you have not been there please see an aspect of yourself there. You may be surprised if this aspect looks different than you, but that can happen. Whatever visual you receive, allow yourself to see it

- Now allow yourself to fully immerse your senses in the place or event. What would it smell like, taste like, feel like? What sort of noises would you hear?
- When you get the sense of the place or event as fully as possible, you will inwardly question if this is a place from your ancestry, past lives, or from a future timeline (meaning either somewhere you will go or need to go, for whatever reason). If you do not get a clear answer, that is fine. This information can be interesting to know, but is not essential to do this work
- Introduce yourself to this aspect of Self. This can be as simple as saying "hello"
- Now, ask what you need to know about this place or event. You may need to revisit this aspect of Self a few times to get a clear answer
- Once you do get an answer of what you should know, ask if this aspect of Self is willing to return to you so you can be fully embodied
- If no, ask what they need to be willing to do so, and either agree to the terms they are giving (this may be something you need to do in your daily, current life) or visualize this aspect receiving what they need
- When they no longer need anything and are willing to return, you will again visualize a cord going from them to you and have them walk into you, picking up the slack of the cord as they go

- When they fully merge with you, you will either utilize the source doorway or the felt sensation of imagery of sunlight to allow for this energy to fully integrate within you

If you are experiencing a call to be in a different land, or to take part in a specific event, you may learn that you are actually intended to be there. You may also learn that you should visit your ancestral homeland, or that a past life had difficulties in a particular place in the world. If there are intense difficulties and this piece is unwilling to come home despite offering help to do so, finding a spiritual worker who does past life work or ancestral work to fully find out their story and what they need to heal may be necessary.

It is much more common for an aspect of Self to be energetically participating in a land or event than an actual cord to the place or event. However, in rare cases we do find ourselves corded to a specific element in nature, a specific land, or an event itself. In some ways this is natural– we naturally form a cord to the place of our homeland, our ancestry, and our birth. This is why we tend to feel more at home in these places, and why people who have come from cultures who migrated or were forced out of lands tend to have a bit of a drifter or unsettled quality to their energy.

We should, in fact, be corded to the Earth in a healthy, balanced way. These cords can be worked with and cleared in case of imbalance, or in case of simply wanting to move away from where we are currently. Cording through the midline (later in this course) will allow for us to be corded to both the Earth and Heavens in a balanced way.

But in some instances we may find that we are corded to an actual place we have visited, a tree, mountain, or cave, or to an actual event without being able to find an aspect of Self there. While this can be entirely natural– we have formed a bond or relationship to something similar to how we cord to people– it is always best to again check the cord, as well as the flow of the cord, to make sure that we are in balance. So if you find yourself from the previous sections unable to find an aspect of Self present, you will do the following:

- Ask to see or sense the cord as well as what it is connected to. This cord may be more difficult to see than some of the others, but you should be able to ask and receive information about the place or event you are connected to.
- Allow yourself to fully immerse yourself in whatever place or event comes up. See, sense, smell, hear… whatever senses arise allow for yourself to paint a full picture of what you are corded to
- Ask your inner guidance or the place/event itself why you are corded to it. Listen for the answer. If you are unable to hear an answer, you can simply go back another day, or you can continue and see what comes up
- Once you come into awareness of why you are corded to a place or event, ask your inner guidance if this is healthy and

balanced or unhealthy and imbalanced to be corded to this place or event
- Is being corded to this place/event depleting you of any energy?
- Is it causing you to feel scattered or to not want to fully participate in your life?
- If it is balanced, you can simply acknowledge what you are connected to. If it feels appropriate, you can even thank it for being a part of you
- You can also ask for the place to "tell you more" about your connection and learn information about yourself in relation to the place or event
- If it is imbalanced, you will ask what you need to do to return this cord to a state of balance. The general options are severing the cord entirely, working with the energetics of the cord so it is balanced, taking care of something in your every-day life, or realizing something about the connection to the place or event
- When you get a sense of what you need to do, ask your inner guidance or ask the place or event what you need to know about your connection
- Once you realize why you are connected and what you need to know about your connection, you can typically do a simple cutting and clearing of the cord from the basic work; or you can adjust the cord as was discussed in the *Altering Cords* section

If the cord will not cut or clear, or you do not gather information about it, it is likely that you simply need to revisit the cord and the place or event a few times to gather information about it. Once you come into full realization of why you are corded to this place or event, the cord will naturally be able to be cut, cleared, or altered.

Again, you may find that the connection or cording is quite natural and appropriate. It may be something that you cherish, or want to keep. It may in fact be something that you want to do information gathering about for several months so that you can learn all of the lessons and realizations about the place or event so it has a deeper impact on your life.

The realization and layers of information that come from being tied to a specific place or event may come more slowly than our cords to another person, or even another aspect of Self. These cords tend to be thicker and tougher with less energy flow than our more interpersonal cords. This is due to land energies generally being of a slower vibration and an obviously more grounded, earth-based nature. It is much more symptomatic from these types of cords to simply feel stuck, or pulled to a place, event, or element in nature, rather than to feel a range of emotions and trauma like our other cording mechanisms. This also means that it may take longer for us to gather information, or have our questions answered. Simply have patience, and realize that some of the cord work will take some time. It is well worth the effort to understand why we are corded to a particular place or event, and the patience we show in visiting with that place, event, and cord many times, or over many months, will allow for us to really understand ourselves at a deeper level and to release layers of underlying patterns and imbalances that we likely never thought were possible.

**Cords to Spirits, Energies and Beings**
A somewhat rare form of cording is to spirits, energies and beings. The most common reason for this is due to a family member, friend, or other human that we likely had a relationship with dying but not fully moving on. When a human in death does not move on to another plane of existence they become earthbound, eventually needing to attach themselves to another source of energy (such as another human) in order to remain present here.

The other type of cording we may run into at an advanced, highly conscious level is cording to energies and beings. These can run the gamut from being corded to a thoughtform, field of energy, or energetic structure to being corded to a being, elemental, or darker presence.

This course is not to argue the existence of many of these types of energies, or a full course on spirit release. Spirit release is extremely important work, but since this course is focused on cording we will consider such events from the perspective of having a cord to an energy or consciousness. Realization that such energies exist, and that we can in fact be corded to them, simply comes from having a heightened level of sensitivity and consciousness. Since this work requires skills, such as spirit release, a highly attuned spiritual state, and very advanced skilled spiritual work, we will approach such cords through understanding, which may be enough in some cases to release the cords. It is critical if you find such cording within yourself or a client to get the appropriate training in working with spirits, beings, or energy fields to be able to fully release both the spirit and the cord. This is to ensure safety and the least amount of chaos for ourselves as well as any clients we may have.

The basic reason that these cords remain or form is because it is a contract that we may have consciously or subconsciously created with the spirit or being. Although it may be an odd thing to think about when first presented with this understanding, we all know of stories of mothers saying they will "always take care of their children". It is common and understandable considering the bond and love that most mothers feel for their children, and the cords between mother and child can be quite complex and multi-layered. But when a child passes away, this contract to always take care of the child may remain, so the child remains earthbound and corded to the mother.

In other cases pacts between soldiers, friends, and partners are readily understandable and can be carried over past physical death. In these cases it is important to release the bond and then the spirit by surrendering the vow or contract we have made in life. Although it is understandable to want to keep a presence around us, especially when it is as sad and difficult as losing a child or a friend during military service, death is intended to be a release. This means that we are intended to move on in death from this plane of existence. Staying here causing difficulty for both the spirit as well as the human who is corded to them– the living person is unable to move through the stages of grief and trauma because they can sense their loved one, friend, or colleague corded and still present with them.

It should be noted that this is quite a difficult subject to broach with clients, and should be done so gently. It is rare that a mother will be ready to let go of her deceased child, even if she understands that it is time for him to move on logically. We are not logical creatures, we make decisions based on emotions. Having compassion for someone who has had a great loss, or who this is occurring to, is crucial. As spiritual workers or energy workers we do not and should not force anyone to let go of anything they are not ready to. By simply having the awareness of this type of cording we can hold space for our clients (and ourselves) and come to the type of gradual realization and readiness that this is an imbalanced situation so we can release the cord and contract we have created.

It is also possible to have contracts with former humans who we do not share an intense bond with. It is the case with small children that they can pick up "imaginary friends" and then forty years later with a lot of training under their belt they realize that this "imaginary friend" was in fact a spirit and is still attached to them. It can be difficult to release a bond to someone who we have known for so long, even if we realize it is harmful. We may have also asked for protection, a friend, or something else and a spirit willingly obliged. It is up to the person who has asked for such things (and formed such a contract) to release the contract and then the former human from their physical body and energy field.

We may also find ourselves corded to a being– such as an elemental, dark presence (such as a shadow person), angel, deity, or archetype– because we in some way created a bond or asked for such an experience. It should be noted that there is a culture in modern day spiritual work of victim-blaming, meaning that we love to believe that anyone who is having difficult spiritual experience is doing so because they in some way "asked for it" or had a lot of darkness. This belief is maintained and passed along by people who live in fear of the spirit world. They maintain illusions such as this so that they can feel comfortable and safe playing in the spiritual realms with the mentality that nothing bad or difficult will happen to them as long as they maintain a positive outlook or "high vibration".

This simply is not true. It is actually true that the higher vibration or more conscious we become the more that we become aware of darker energies– either to help, or simply because we see more of the spectrum of the universe and are more aware of the spirit world than most people are. The more conscious we become, in fact, the easier it is for us to have all sorts of energies gravitate towards us, or even attempt to cord to us.

In some cases we may have asked for something interesting to happen to us, or worked with magic, occult material, or spiritual work that was beyond us. We may have simply been lonely and wished for a friend. All of these are contracts that may have provided an opening for a being of some sort to take us up on our wish and to form a contract or bond with us. By becoming increasingly conscious we can realize what or who is in our bodies and our field and take care of it on the appropriate level.

Although what we have gone over is seemingly of a more negative or darker nature, we can also find ourselves having contracts to angels, deities, and what we commonly think of as benevolent presences. In rare cases we may find ourselves corded to a powerful energy, and in some cultures a spirit marriage, or bond created where we are married to a spirit or deity, creates a vow and bond that can be difficult to break. This type of marriage is done through ceremony or offerings traditionally, but we may find ourselves entering into a spirit marriage without ceremony or even full recognition of quite what we are doing.

In extremely rare cases we may find ourselves corded to a specific dimension, layer of spirit, collective consciousness, archetype, energy field, or thoughtform. These cases require an extremely competent, experienced, and aware spiritual worker or energy worker to both clear the cording mechanism as well as release whatever we are attached to.

In all of these cases, realization that we are corded to something that is not in any of the other categories– to living humans, a part of ourselves, place or event– may come up. We may be sensitive and aware and have already had this realization, or we may come to this realization after doing a lot of cord work in the previous categories and realizing that there are cords left. By becoming aware of these cords we can go to an advanced spiritual worker or energy worker to release the spirit and the contract, or we may choose to move on to learning how to release spirits ourselves.

    If we do have experience with spirits, beings, and other energies, and know how to release them properly and fully we can become aware of the contract involved, discovering at what age it was created and what the contract actually is. We can then have our client (or ourselves) renounce the contract at both their current age and then the age that the contract was created. It helps if the client does this out loud for the proper emphasis. It is only then that methods of spirit release will be effective. This is a commonly missed part of spirit release, and the client will simply have the spirit or being return because of the cording mechanism, even if we have (or think we have) cleared them or moved on the being or spirit.

    If we have a tremendous amount of experience with energy fields, we can find out what exactly the client is hooked into or corded to, find and return any aspect of Self that may be present there, and have a spiritual helper unhook them from the field. You would then do a basic dissolving of the cord into sunlight, and require that the client do not participate or even think (as much as possible) about the energy field, dimension, or universe that they were hooked into. This happens most frequently with astral travelers who are unskilled and are unable to find their way back to their bodies, but it can also simply happen for a variety of odd reasons that are particular to that individual and their energetic makeup.

**Part Two**

Now that we have fully explored how to work with cords stemming from our current selves, we will begin working with cording to our past lives, our ancestry, and our future or destiny line.

These cords are considered "natural" cords– meaning that they are intended to be there and are a natural part of our energetic blueprint. So our focus has gone from clearing, cutting, or altering to simply understanding, working with, and perhaps healing energies that are within cords. It is by sitting in realization of these cords and learning how to work with or "travel" them that we can uncover layers of ourselves, become more awake, and heal patterns that have a large impact on our outward lives.

It is not until we reach a certain level of consciousness that we become fully cognizant of just how many patterns, belief systems, traumas, and energies are passed down to us. It is by understanding and healing the energies that are within such cords that we can fully become who we are intended to be– and to awaken to the point of freeing ourselves, no longer mindlessly following the patterns, traumas, and belief systems that have been passed down to us without question. Awakening is a state of freedom– where we are able to look at our past, and the many layers of Self, and to surrender what is not vitally us. It is only through awareness, understanding, and healing of the wounds and subconscious patterns that we are mindlessly reenacting in our current lives that we can fully reclaim our lives as our own. Working with the cords is a powerful way to understand ourselves and to rise above these beliefs and traumas that have been passed down to us.

There are many ways to work with ancestral trauma and past lives that have emerged over the last few decades. Some different way of working with these I have detailed in my book *The Spiritual Awakening Guide: Kundalini, Psychic Abilities, and the Conditioned Layers of Reality* if you find yourself wanting more information on the subject. But through working with our cording mechanism we can perhaps have a different perspective that will allow us to understand and heal differently than through the utilization of other methods.

**Ancestral Lineage Cord**

When we consider the entirety of our family tree there are many branches and perhaps many different countries and cultures that we originate from. In terms of spiritually working with ancestors it can be an approach to explore each of those branches and discover the folk, magical, and spiritual traditions of each one. The connections, guidance, and abilities that we can discover through our ancestors is an important step for any serious spiritual worker in order to cultivate spiritual knowledge and power. Likewise, learning how to do ancestral healing, particularly the clearing and resolution of ancestral trauma, can have an indelible impact on our lives. Overall, working with the ancestors themselves (our own or more generally) can be an essential spiritual practice that brings strength, power, and understanding to anyone who chooses (or has been chosen) to work with them.

Our ancestral cord is a bit different. We are composed of different cords in our energetic anatomy as a part of our blueprint. Our blueprint is how energies come together for the purposes of this lifetime. We like to consider ourselves as separate "bodies"- spiritual, energetic, and physical- but really we are a grouping of energies and energetic structures that come together for the purposes of our present incarnation on Earth. These energies form around a blueprint- or how a human being should be formed energetically, physically, mentally, and spiritually.

In this course we are primarily going to concern ourselves with the spiritual blueprint and the cording mechanisms that naturally come from us to connect us to our spiritual natures and outer spiritual reality. There are many of these cords that inform who we are and connect us to one another, to our other "bodies" (explored in the next section), and to the energetic lines that feed us information and energy. Our energetic blueprint is a grid of energy, composed of lines, cords, and dots that we can learn to work with to achieve better health, vitality, and greater spiritual understanding. Although cords are but a small part of our overall energetic blueprint, they are essential to learn how we connect to energies that are of a greater spiritual nature and that inform our physical existence.

Through this chapter specifically we will be working with the ancestral cord– a typically tough, membranous, and large cord that connects us to the entirety of our ancestral line. We will then work with the past life cord and the destiny line. All of these cords inform our present incarnation and allow for us to feel anchored into a specific time and space. We may come to the realization that constructs such as present, past, and future are illusory– and that we are made up of both future, ancestral, and past life energies and patterns that are living through us in our current incarnation. Even if we are not yet at that realization, we can still work with these structures and have a positive impact on our lives by doing so.

*The Ancestral Cord*

As mentioned, the ancestral cord is tough in texture, large, and contains a significant amount of energy. Many of my clients who have done this work have reported sightings or sensations of blood vessels within the cord, or have seen the flow of energy through this cord be of the texture, consistency, or color of blood. This is due the fact that ancestral energies run through our bloodstream. There are many cultures that will do ceremonies, for example, connecting the spiritual gifts of the ancestry through blood or wine, which is an obvious and common representation of blood.

The ancestral cord is typically found emanating from the back of the body on the midline somewhere between around the area of where the top part of our sacrum (the triangle-shaped bone) meets our lower back. It is anchored deeply, is quite large, and is common to have many twists and turns, thorns, vines, plant-like structures, blood vessels, or crater and volcanic-type imagery.

This cord can only be found through personal exploration and direct experience. The way that this cord is "worked" with is to become aware of it. Although it seems simplistic, even becoming aware of a deep, energetic structure such as this can change our lives. We must be prepared to be able to sense it spiritually, mentally, and physically. If you are not able to sense it, it just means that it is not quite the right time for you to yet. Simply come back to this work in a few weeks, or a few months, and check again.

However, to work with this cord you will:

- First, allow yourself to realize that you have a cord that connects you to your ancestry. This is a single, thick cord that will feel like it is coming straight out from your back, and most likely your spine or sacrum (the triangle shaped bone in your lower back)
- If you have not already begun to discover, feel, or in some way sense a cord, allow for your eyes to gently close, take a few breaths, and ask for this cord to appear. Say that you are ready to see and sense it
- If you are still not able to sense it, completely close your eyes and imagine yourself in a dark room with only a single

candle burning. Allow yourself to gently look at the flame. This flame will gently begin to highlight your energetic blueprint and many cords. Gently ask which is the ancestral cord
- Come back to your body and do a body scan, asking to sense this cord
- If you are unable to find it through any of these methods, it may not be quite the right time for you to see this. Continue to do cord work and personal development work, such as meditation, and you will likely remember this meditation at the right time for you to again approach this work

This work should allow for you, if you are ready, to discover- in some way sense, feel, or visualize- this cord. It is perfectly fine if you discover the cord lower on your body, slightly off midline, or different in color or size than what others have reported. If you are able to get even a vague sense of the cord, you can continue:

- Fully allow for your focus to go to this cord
- How deep does it feel in your body?
- How would you describe it? Describe the size, texture, color, felt sense, or anything else that comes up about the cord
- When you have a strong sense of the cord, allow yourself to feel the strength and vibrancy of the cord. Does it seem strong and vibrant with a clear flow of energy?

- Let yourself look for or sense this cord leaving your body. Does it curve, snake, or is it straight?
- Let yourself look for or sense the cord itself as far as you are able to going out of your body. Sit with the felt sense of visual of this cord for a few moments
- Now imagine yourself or sense yourself as being at the spot where the cord emanates out of your body. You can imagine yourself as anything that you want– just simply energy, a miniaturized version of yourself, or something else entirely
- Travel down the length of the cord as it goes away from your body. Only go as far as you were able to get a sense of while examining the cord prior
- How does the cord look? Are there any dark spots, knots, places where it is not flowing?
- How is the energy of the cord? Is it flowing slowly but smoothly or is the flow choppy, stagnant, or can you not sense the flow at all?
- Can you sense an emotion in the cord? Or a few emotions?

Ideally the cord will have a smooth, slow flow with even color, texture, and size. It is completely natural if it loops or twists, but it should not have knots, kinks, or any type of blockage. You should not have any strong emotions come up while examining the cord– this would indicate needs for healing at the ancestral level. If you do have strong emotions arise, allowing them to simply release from you or in some way lift off the cord, similar to the prior sections, is all that typically needs to be done.

Although it is natural for us to want to "do" a lot with cords we simply do not have to here. If we are at the point of being able to sense and sit with this cord we will have emotional, spiritual, and energetic releases occur simply because we are awake and aware enough to be cognizant of such a structure. The further that we get to the blueprint or more "spiritual" levels of existence the less we have to do. By sitting with and learning how to travel the length of the cord we will naturally come to a state of balance with the energies that we are discovering, and our ancestral line as a whole. New events, realizations, understandings, and circumstances in our outer lives will appear as we sit with this cord, simply and directly focusing on it.

When we put focus and realization towards this cord we may find memories, patterns, and emotions rising that are releasing from our ancestral line. Some of these may seem strange to us, and we may experience odd dreams, a range of emotions that may be overwhelming, or simply a realization that the patterns that we used to unthinkingly enact in our daily lives repeatedly or belief systems we carry may be a result of deeper energies than just our selves and this incarnation.

This is completely to be expected as we sit with this cord, and we can just surrender these experiences, memories, and emotions as they arise. It is important to ask the question "is this ancestral" when we experience such things so our inner self can say "yes" or "no" and we do not think that we are crying for no reason, or suddenly find ourselves faced with a night or two of dream-filled sleep with seemingly no cause.

It is natural (and understandably a bit frustrating) to list a meditation that not everyone will be able to complete right away. Some of these deeper energetic structures require a certain level of persistence, patience, and level of consciousness. However, even by reading about structures like this on some level your body and consciousness will begin to prepare you to some day be able to fully understand and explore this work.

**Cords to Past Lives**

When we begin to become aware of past lives we may initially believe that past incarnations are in fact in the past and are simply influencing our present state. We may find out while exploring past lives why we are frightened of the water, or what the constriction in our throat is, or that we have a fear of men or women based on something deeper than this current incarnation. This course will teach you about how to work with cords to past lives, and to the past lifeline, but the basics of past lives, why they remain, and how they show up for us in our physical body are best found in my book *The Spiritual Awakening Guide*.

We may also go beyond this, realizing that we are not only influenced by past lives– and the patterns, traumas, and beliefs of our past selves– but that we are currently experiencing many different timelines at once, and are experiencing many different lifetimes concurrently. Many of us do not come to this understanding because it is difficult to logically process. We like clean, linear logic and to think of time as a straight line because it is simpler on our brains and how we each individually construct our reality to do so. Most of us are only experiencing a very small spectrum of our physical, energetic, and spiritual selves, even if we are interested in a spiritual path.

Until we recognize that we are experiencing lives simultaneously, we may enjoy working with parts of ourselves in different incarnations similarly to how the cord work was done in the *Cording to Places and Events* section. We would ask for a past life cord to highlight, follow it out, and create a visual of our Self in our past incarnation. We would then ask that incarnation what they would need to heal, to release emotions, or to simply be okay. We would then imagine that for them or offer that to them. The cord to that incarnation should automatically dissolve if the past life is healed. If it is not, we can allow for that past life to slowly walk into our physical bodies, merging with us. We would then use the source doorway method or the sunlight method to fully dissolve the card and re-integrate the past life into our bodies.

*The Past Life Line*

If we want information about our past lives, one of the simplest ways to discover such information is through the past life line, or cord. Through this cord we can go back to our previous lives to learn about them as well as discover any patterns or deaths that need further healing work done.

This line is a dark silver cord that will emanate from somewhere between the back of the heart and the base of the neck. It typically looks like a woven cord and has an electric look and feel to it. As we sit with the cord, discovering it in the same way as the Ancestral cord, we will find that as we travel down it that it naturally has knots in it. These knots are formed in each of our lives, and can be simply counted down. By this I mean that the first knot will represent your most recent past life, the next knot the life before that, and so on. It is typical for even the most sensitive and aware person to get at most three knots, especially at first.

To fully work with this line first you will discover it as you did the ancestral line. You will then sit with it, remarking on color, size, texture, any physical sensations you notice, and what you intuitively sense about the cord. You are welcome to also utilize the traveling method discussed in the Ancestral cording section. You will then continue to discover more about the cord:

- When you have gotten a strong felt sense or visual about the cord, get a sense of how far you can notice or sense it extend in back or around you
- Now, sit with the cord and sense or see if you can see any knots. You will do this by first focusing on the cord where it rises out from your body and then following it until you notice a knot or bump in the cord

- This knot or bump is your first past life, meaning the last time you were incarnated
- If you are able to notice a knot, allow for all of your focus to go to that knot. Sit in a space of gentle noticing of that knot for a few moments
- You will then ask for that knot to gently release. It may also do so on its own
- If it does not, you will ask for a known spiritual helper that you have to untie the knot. If you feel comfortable, you can untie the knot yourself as well
- When you do this, if done correctly, an image, scent, sound, or felt sense will emerge of that past life
- Notice everything that you can about the scene, what you look like, and what may be happening
- The knot will naturally begin to re-tie itself after a period of time

Over a period of time the length of time that the knot will stay untied will become longer and you will get more sights, sounds, and realizations from the past life. When this past life has been healed (meaning that the manner of death has been reconciled, and any traumas or emotions that are still lurking resolve) the knot will fully be undone.

    It is not necessary to fully move on (or untie) a knot before you move on to the next one. You may be able to visit two or three "knots" at a time, gathering information. It is more a question of focus than anything– we tend to not be able to maintain and stay in these sorts of liminal spaces for lengthy periods of time.

As we work through our past lives and heal them we will be able to go further back our past life line. It is typical of us to stop ourselves before we get too far– we only wish to know so much information or heal so much of ourselves. It is also natural to stop at the end of human incarnations. We may have had many lifetimes as various animals, or some lifetimes where we were not such a pleasant person, which caused a karmic reaction to pass forward into its future incarnations. Animal lives tend to be much shorter, with much less baggage, so beyond the ego not wanting to imagine ourselves as anything but human, we may only get a quick glimpse at a past life as an animal, insect, plant, or energy.

Healing past lives can be revolutionary for our current incarnation. With each knot we have the opportunity to learn about the originator of many of our beliefs, understandings, and patterns. We can again heal them by simply asking what they need and working through them as if they were a separate "client" from us, or we may want to take the information we gather from untying our knots to a spiritual worker who specializes in past lives to assist us in the healing process.

## Cording to the Future Self and Destiny Line

It is much easier for us to reconcile mentally that we have past lives and ancestors that are currently having an impact on our current selves than to have realization or understanding of our future selves or future incarnations. There are likely reasons why- as we are a culture for the most part who tends to think of time as being a linear construct, and we commonly and collectively understand that the forces of the past create the present. We also may not like to think about the future due to our cultural fears around getting older (this varies by culture to some extent) and death.

There are many people who are able to reconcile those fears and open up to the realization that we can work with our future selves and our destiny line. Similar to the past life cord, the destiny cord is a single cord that emanates from us. Rather than being attached to (or through) our physical body it seems to be, in most people, in the space of the heart approximately six inches out. It is a strong but gossamer looking cord with many different threads coming together that surround the cord, going through the inside lining of the heart chakra. Others have reported this cord emanating from the solar plexus, and due to this work being highly experiential it is impossible at this date to determine why or how the location may vary like this.

The way to find the location of this structure through your own direct experience is the same method as is found in the *Ancestral Cord* section, with one variation. If you are able to feel or sense your heart chakra, I suggest gently focusing on that first, and then looking for or sensing a spiral of gossamer threads. You will then simply wait, keeping focus on those threads, until they form a cord. This cord should flow through the chakra and ideally would be one cord with a lot of different fibers creating it. If this is the first or second time you have done this meditation it is typical for those fibers to not make a cohesive cord mechanism. This means that the typical person who is able to do this work will only be able to see or sense many different shimmering threads within their heart chakra going outward.

If you are not able to see these threads, or the threads do not form a cohesive unit, you can patiently sit with the knowledge that the "destiny threads" are there and meditate on the space until it is time or you are prepared to find them. It is much more common for you to need to work through understanding and working with other energetic structures, reaching a specific level of energetic and spiritual attainment, to see these structures than it is for there to be something wrong with the destiny line itself. However, if you do sit with these structures and feel like something is wrong, a visit to a very experienced spiritual worker who can do future work, or destiny retrieval, is recommended.

Once these tendrils or thread-like structures are found, you can continue:

- Sit with the thread-like structures and ask for them to become clear and enter into a state of balance
- You can simply sit and observe these threads. The simple act of realizing that they are there is often enough to have a shift in your awareness and to further understand your path
- If you are ready, you can simply communicate with either the threads or the singular cord. You can ask questions like:

- - What should I know about my destiny in this lifetime?
  - What should I know about my path currently?
  - What should I know in general?
- You are welcome to ask any questions that you like. Answers may not come straight away– you may need to ask a few times or wait and look for occurrences, messages, and synchronicities in your life after doing this meditation

At some point you may come to the realization that the future or destiny line forms a sort of woven tapestry, or grid. This is typically after the threads have come together to form a single cord. As you sit and contemplate the cord you will see the finely woven nature of it– and how disparate threads come together from all different types of sources to form the cord.

If you are able to travel the cord, as was discussed in the prior section, you will find yourself in a completely white space. It is in this space that you are able to meet your guardian angel. If you are reading this section intellectually, there is likely disbelief on your part that this can happen, or does happen. That is totally understandable and expected until you are able to have direct experience of some of the things I am teaching. Teaching this work over the past few years I would say that out of fifty or students that I felt were ready for this type of work about five or ten were able to eventually travel this cord into a completely white space, or room, without my telling them prior about such a space existing.

While in this room you will simply ask for your guardian angel, spirit, or being. This is an intelligence that knows about your energetic makeup, your current incarnation, and your future. When you are ready, this being will appear. Ensure that you feel safe and intuitively feel like this is the correct energy coming forward. Also act the energy if they are your guardian angel. If they say "yes" and you feel a strong intuitive sense that this is correct, you can continue.

It bears repeating that this work is incredibly advanced and that our tendency is to want the highest, most advanced experiences to happen, and to happen quickly. But even getting to the point of noticing the threads in this work is highly advanced work that only a very small percentage of the population will be able to sense or see.

When we come into contact with our guardian angel, we will naturally fall into line with them energetically. This basically means that we can never go back from not knowing that we have such a teacher and guide in our lives. We can approach this relationship as we would any spiritual relationship, traveling to the white room to communicate with this intelligence, or we may choose to bring this energy into our every-day lives. We do this by working with the destiny line, simply sitting with it and watching it expand, contract, and pulsate as it naturally does.

By simply sitting with this energetic structure we will be in full cosmic flow– meaning that its energies will be able to directly inform us and influence our lives– and we will be able to feel the natural tides, flows, and energies that come through it. By awakening the destiny line, you will come into full realization of who you are now, what you are intended to do, and come into line with who you are intended to be.

It should be noted that the destiny line can take us far beyond our own incarnation. We may eventually have the opportunity to follow this line out, similar to the past lives line, to see our future incarnations. Although this may seem like an interesting or even wonderful thing to do, there are cautions about opening too many spiritual doors, or sources of spiritual knowledge for ourselves. Although it may seem strange to those who have not experienced it, the realization of future and past incarnations, or the Self in other dimensions simultaneously causes us to be permanently split. This means that we will be viewing our lives as if watching several different televisions at once. This is obviously difficult to reconcile for even the sanest or most balanced mind. So if you do begin to stumble across your Self in future incarnations, I would suggest not probing too deeply and not opening a spiritual door that would likely be best shut.

*Journey to the Future Self*
Although this is a book on cording, I frequently get asked about traveling to visit the Self five or ten years in the future. I do not suggest that people travel beyond that for obvious reasons. Traveling to the future Self can be done via the destiny cord, but it is not suggested because it seems to lack the precision of the knots

of the past life cord, and it can be easy to not have certainty about where or what time knowledge is coming from in the future.

Because of this, and because it is a frequent source of interest amongst many people, I am bringing in a classic shamanic journey to visit and learn from your future self in this incarnation.

- First, you are going to journey to a beach. This is a calm beach with a beautiful ocean breeze and sand. It is an empty beach– only you will be there
- Now, you are going to look for a cave. This will be an above ground cave (as in it doesn't go under the earth). It will stretch horizontally
- Enter the cave.
- In the cave you will see a path that goes down into the Earth to the left and one that stays above ground directly in front of you or slightly towards your right. Go towards the right pathway
- Before you walk along this path, question if you want to meet your future Self five or ten years in the future
- After you do this, saying something like "I wish to meet myself five years in the future", begin to walk down the path
- To your right and left you will see doorways, or inlets. Walk until one has significance to you. This doorway may look

- different, or feel like it is pulling you in, or you may walk past it and then realize that you should go back to it
- Walk through the doorway. Through this doorway will be your Self five years in the future
- First, simply take in the environment they are in
- Then, simply say hello. They will realize you are coming because you have already done this
- You may simply want to stay at a basic introductory or questioning stage this time, or the first many times
- You can keep any questions clear and concise:
  - What should I know?
  - What should I know about my path right now?
  - What should I do about my career?
- Any and all questions about your life here on Earth (meaning finances, career, romance, spiritual path, and so forth) you are welcome to ask. Do not worry if you do not receive an answer– it may simply not be the right time for you to know certain information
- At some point you may wish to have her merge with you. She will do this by walking straight into you. You would do this by asking her if it is the right time and for her explicit permission
- You will know that you have done this correctly when you feel her with you, or you start to have understandings and realizations that are beyond your current level. This first

often begins as a distinct knowledge of what you should be doing or how you should be doing it- a sort of confidence
- When you are done with your journey, say thank you, and then walk out of the doorway and down the same path you come out onto the beach.
- You can then open your eyes and write down what she said, or simply reflect on the experience

**Part Three**

In this section we will now begin focusing on cords that connect the varying pieces of ourselves to the cosmos and the Earth. In modern spiritual and energetic circles, the focus of learning about our energetic anatomy tends to be on the chakra system. While chakras can certainly be important to learn about, other energies in the body- such as the meridians, kundalini, ovals, grids, and our energetic blueprints- are just as important and rarely discussed.

We begin by discussing the midline cord, which is the column of energy that flows through our midline and connects us to the Earth as well as the Heavens. In occult literature this can be similar in scope to the Middle Pillar, and in energy work can be similar to the source doorway we discussed previously. Working with the midline cord allows for us to become deeply rooted in the Earth as well as to receive clear input from cosmic sources, both of which will allow us to enter a state of power, grace, and flow. When we are able to enter into flow our lives naturally take on a state of ease, and we are able to handle the difficulties that life will inevitably throw at us in a much different manner than we likely used to. After we have accomplished finding and working with our midline cord we may find that the "Heaven" cord that goes up above our heads can lead us to an expanded cord, known as the cosmic or universal cord, that will connect us with the many different layers of the cosmos.

We then will delve into cords attaching our energy bodies to one another. Although we have many more than five bodies– physical, astral, etheric, mental, and spiritual– for the purposes of this course we will be referring to that structure and understanding. By realizing how we are connected we can take command of our energy bodies, our lives, and of our physical container in a profound way.

This section ends with the extremely important work of navigating the birth cord. It should come as no shock to advanced energetic and spiritual workers that our time in utero is of profound importance to our life here on Earth. By learning how to clear this cord of trauma we can let go of things like resistance to incarnation and deeply charged belief systems, as well as be able to fully accept our physical bodies and our lives in a way we likely never thought we could.

**The Midline Cord**
In Chinese Medicine the midline is referred to as the channels it is composed of– the du and the ren. These channels are some of the first to develop in utero, and are considered "extraordinary" due to

their depth and importance. Other forms of energy work and spiritual healing, such as Qi Gong, focus on the midline and the observation of moving of energy through these channels. The midline is where such primal energies as Kundalini and its accompanying channels Ida and Pingala emerge and spiral around. In occult literature the "Middle Pillar" exercise is still popular with many serious practitioners.

If we study any spiritual, energetic, occult, or bodywork method seriously we are likely to realize the significance of the midline. However, in most of these methods the work done is contained within the body– meaning the cycling of energies within the human container. It is rare to work with the central column, or midline, that extends out above the head and goes below the feet.

Through this work we will open a doorway directly to source. Rather than a specific "cord" what will reveal to us is a column of light that goes through our heads, down through our midline, and deep into the Earth. The more focus and experience we have with this meditation the more we will be able to realize a divine presence here on Earth. We will also be able to radiate this light to whomever and whatever we choose.

Since it is source energy of the highest vibration it will naturally begin to bring up things in ourselves that are calling out for healing. This is something to be aware of as we are working with higher vibration and more cosmic sources of energy. It is typical to work with an energy like this and enter a flow state where we completely realize oneness, or our own divinity, and then to come crashing down to Earth when we come out of such a space. This process is referred to as "flickering" where our "ordinary" baseline state may still contain a fair amount of grief, depression, anger, or fear. As we work with higher energies and have more expanded experiences when we flicker back to our ordinary baseline the emotions that arise (of grief, fear, depression, and so forth) may be difficult for us to understand at first.

If we simply allow for ourselves to release whatever is coming up without question we can clear a great deal of unresolved trauma and emotion through higher experiences. When we begin to resolve a great deal of these emotions our baseline will no longer be as low, and we will not experience the same intensity of emotions, or such a huge difference between our ordinary, every day state and the state we are in while exploring expanded or cosmic consciousness.

While working with clients we can simply radiate this light towards them so that they can experience it. For anyone who is able to experience and cultivate this column of light the amount of light and energy that you are able to experience is in some ways indescribable. If done right, you will be directly in flow– beyond the layers of illusory and constructed reality– and be able to feel the ebbs and flows of the cosmic ocean itself run through you.

As a word of caution, if this work does bring up needs for healing for you, it is best to find an experienced healer before proceeding again. This is a deceptively simple meditation with profound implications. Doing this work too much, or proceeding despite warning signs from your body that you should perhaps take a break, can result in a state of spiritual emergency. This is not to scare, as this is a meditation that will take a bit of time to accomplish properly, despite its simplicity. What is simply to be stated here (as it would be or should be with much of the advanced work) is that if you are already feeling unstable or imbalanced in your life it is often best to pursue body-based methods– exercise, walking, yoga, gardening– before exploring too much of the spiritual or energetic.

- At first you will bring your focus to the Heavens. You can imagine yourself growing taller to reach them so that you do not travel out of your physical body
- When you have reached an appropriate height you will see or sense a globe of light. This is different than the chakras above your head– it will be several miles up and generally be more brilliant. It may be difficult to look at directly
- Allow for this globe of light to open– radiating energy down through your crown and midline. If you do this correctly, a column of light will appear from the Heavens, through the top of your head, and down into your pelvis
- Now, allow for your focus to go to a similar sphere deep within the Earth. Again, this is different than chakras below your feet– this will feel like a primal, strong energy that has nothing to do with your own energetic system

- Allow for the light that has created a column through you to pass through your genitals and in between your legs to meet up with this sphere. If you are ungrounded, this energy may not feel fully connected at first
- If you have not already, imagine yourself shrinking back down to normal size with a complete column of light flowing through you

It is completely normal at first to not have a full, vibrant column of light. Although this energy may wish to radiate outwards from the column shape, it is best to keep your focus on the midline until you are able to sense the full column. The full column should be smoothly flowing with no stops, fuzzy places, or missing sections. It will extend from way above your head to a long distance below your feet. Simply sitting with this column without forcing it to do anything will allow for it to gently break through many blockages. If you do have major blockages (areas where this light will not penetrate) it is best to see a body-based healer, such as an Acupuncturist or CranioSacral therapist, to get energy moving in that area.

Once you have a fully flowing column of light, you can continue:

- With your fully flowing column of light you will allow for it to naturally emanate outward. While most of the energy will remain in your central line, there will naturally be a flow

- outward once it has free flow, strength, and the basic ability to do so
- Watch as it radiates to every cell in your body. Do not force it to move- allow for it to have its own pathways and movement
- If there is a part of your body that you wish to send this light to, gently bring your focus to that area. Say what that area is, for example: "pelvis"
- The light will naturally move in that area. You do not need to force it
- Eventually the light will radiate out of your feet and hands. At this point you can radiate this energy towards anything you choose- clients, plants, items, for spiritual, energetic, or magical purposes.

Once this light naturally radiates from the hands it can be focused to attune objects, spiritual baths, households, lands- really anything that seems like it could use an influx of divine energy. Over time this energy will build and the radiating waves from the midline will create stronger amounts of light coming from your hands, as well as from your whole body. When it becomes stronger this light also has the ability to clear and protect- such as in the creation of protective objects (like talismans), or clearing of spirits from households or land. As we grow our light we will find that we have less to "do" if we have a healing practice, and we will find that the struggles and inconveniences of our lives no longer have the same amount of significance as they once did to us.

It is important that when we get to the phase of directing energy that we consider permission first. Because this energy will bring up anything that is not "divine" it may cause a person to feel sick. They also, for whatever reason, may not wish to receive energy from us or may not be ready to heal. It is best to ask for permission from whatever we are sending this energy to. Everything around us has consciousness, and can be asked if it would like directed energy towards it. Once we permanently have this light emanating from us people, objects, and so forth will naturally be attuned to us simply by our presence. Although we may still wish to occasionally direct energy, in many cases we will find that there is less and less for us to "do" in order to heal, send energy, or even clear.

**How to Work with the Cosmic or Universal Cord**
When we begin to work with the energetic structures above our head we may begin to see a ladder or corded structure. Similar to the destiny line, this structure does not begin in the physical body. It most commonly emanates from what many people consider to be the tenth chakra– or two chakras above the crown chakra. As we focus on this chakra, we are likely to begin to sense the cosmic or universal cord. This cord allows for us to directly connect to the many different levels of spiritual reality. Although the levels that this ladder goes up are seemingly different for each person that

experiences them, it is common to find several similar worlds from explorations done through this ladder.

The first worlds to discover are the varying spiritual "schools" in which we may find spiritual teachers. It is most common to reach these levels by dreaming. It is common for many of us in the beginning or even intermediate stages of awakening to have dreams about being taught in these schools. As we progress we may even find ourselves teaching in these same schools. When it comes to the appropriate time and we come to the appropriate consciousness in our waking reality, we will remember what we were taught in these schools.

The other common world to discover is a museum-type world where we can discover information about ourselves. Since this experience varies for everyone, I am not going to go into detailed descriptions about what can be found there, but people have reported viewing different versions of humanity, different worlds, and all sorts of different beings. Some report being able to access a library where spiritual information that is not commonly realized on Earth is located, or books whose contents are about their individual past, present, or future.

If we are able to climb this ladder or cord to the top we begin to feel sunlight, and will find ourselves in the white space that was referred to in the destiny line chapter. The experience of this sunlight was remarked upon by the ten or so people who were able and conscious enough to find this ladder and climb it to the top without my mentioning it.

Rather than tell you further of what you will experience, since it is seemingly so variable and there is so much territory unexplored, the focus of this section will be on simply finding the cord. It will be up to you to have the direct experience of finding it, climbing it, and discovering what is beyond spiritual doors that not many have been able to explore.

- Once the midline pillar has been fully formed, you will first feel or visualize your crown chakra
- Now, you will begin to see or feel the torus of light that emanates from it
- This light will create an oval shape that reaches the next chakra. Bring your focus to that lighted sphere and gently bring your gaze to the top of that sphere. This is your next chakra
- This chakra will encircle your head as well as will bring a straight vertical light into the chakra above it
- Allow for your focus to come to this chakra. At first all you may see is light, but on gentle examination you may find a ladder or cord-like structure going above it
- If you are able to find this structure, visualize a small version of yourself at the bottom of the cord
- You will then climb the cord until you find a point of interest, doorway, or other structure you wish to have direct experience of

- If you leave the cord or ladder, please be sure to in some way mark how to get back to the cord, or at the very least remember how to get back to it in case where you get off has a closing door, or is confusing.
- When you are ready, climb back down the cord and ensure you are back in your body. You can do this by stomping your feet, getting some exercise, or having a friend who does similar work check to ensure you are back fully.

Since this is a complex meditation with interesting effects, it is often best to have a companion. Take turns discovering and working with this meditation, and have your friend shake you or have the ability to journey to find you in case you get lost or turned around. If doing alone, it is best to set an alarm so that you are not away for too long. It can be easy to come to and realize that instead of the minutes you thought you were gone it is several hours later.

Do not do this work if you are severely disassociated in your normal existence, or are not in a decently balanced psychological state. It can be difficult to find practitioners who can track you to some of these places, so even if it seems easy to simply get off of the ladder to explore a doorway and path that lies before you, always ensure that you look at the doorway, the path that you take, and items around you so that you can take the same route back.

It is typical of people to find doorways, clouds, or other structures that will welcome them to many worlds off of the ladder. When you are ready you can climb to the top and experience the sunlight and then the white space. It should be remarked upon that even realizing that these structures exist can be life changing, and a simple, fun projection up a ladder can propel you much further into spiritual realization than you may think.

Although I am offering a lot of warnings and admonitions, it is likely that if you are not ready, you simply will not see the ladder or rope to climb. It is also likely that if you are not ready you will think that this section is out of your comfort zone, that you are not prepared yet, or that I am crazy. It is likely that you are only interested in this work if you are prepared for some of it, or will be some day. So allow yourself to come to a state of readiness gently, and do not force understandings or further realizations. If you are able to experience only your crown chakra and put a bit of focus there, eventually you will experience more of it and be able to work towards seeing or sensing the one above it. So have patience, and realize that even sitting with the crown chakra can have profound benefits.

**How to Work with Your Etheric and Astral Cord**
The next two cords begin with the grid system of our body. We are composed of many bodies– physical, etheric, astral, and spiritual– which can all be worked with individually through the grid. This is not a discourse on the etheric and astral layers of the body or their functions. For the sake of simplicity, we will say that as we get further away from the physical body we come to many other "bodies". Our etheric is closest to our physical body and essentially

takes the same shape as our physical body. Our astral body is further than this, and is more of an oval type shape with many clouds or colors. As we go further away from the physical body, our energy bodies lose the shape of our physical body and generally become more ovate. This does have some variance, as we may have tears, variances in the grid, or other imbalances in our energy bodies that create a variance from the typical oval shape.

The etheric and astral bodies both have a world, or a few worlds that can be explored through travel outside of the body. My current direct experience, and that of others who have the ability and skills to differentiate between etheric and astral level experiences suggest that the etheric shares not only the shape of our human body but basically the same world as well. The astral body is divided into two parts or worlds– the lower and upper astral– but can have innumerable experiences and places to travel within them since it is not tied to this world in the same way the etheric body is.

Through this section we will discuss the basics of finding the cord to these structures as well as the basics of traveling through them. There are many wonderful books on astral traveling that go into far greater detail on safety and details of the traveling experience. Since this book is centered on the cording mechanisms, we will have our primary focus be on explaining how to find the etheric and astral cords, which can then be utilized for out of body experiences.

As mentioned before, there is a cord that connects our energy bodies together. Each of our "bodies" is actually an electric grid that is full of energetic information and spiritual realizations that can be cultivated. The same cord that connects these bodies goes outward, connecting us to our eternal spiritual nature. This will become clearer as we gain direct experience of this cord.

The etheric/astral cord releases our consciousness through the cord during the state of death. It is silver and at first may appear rather dense. Some describe this cord as a "tunnel" rather than a cord, due to popular spiritual revelations of tunnels being seen in near death experiences.

This cord hooks into the grid systems of the differing layers of our bodies and slightly narrows, creating a tunnel of energy. Only the most advanced practitioners who are ready to work through such fears as physical death will be able to find this cording mechanism. In death, our consciousness flows through this cord and the cord itself gradually loosens from our physical body, allowing our consciousness to go through the cord completely and again find the white space we have referred to in previous chapters.

The cord itself is something that once viewed cannot be un-viewed. This means that simply feeling or sensing this cord will have a profound impact on our lives and will have the effect of bringing up and reconciling our fears surrounding physical death. It will also have the side-effect of allowing for us to travel outside of our bodies easily, if that is something that we wish to do, and to choose which "body" (etheric or astral) and which world we wish to travel in. They each have their distinct advantages, but since astral travel allows for us to lose the emotions and restrictions of our world and our body more fully, most people choose astral travel rather than etheric.

- To find this cord first we must focus on our physical body and our torso specifically
- Allow yourself to feel energy flow through your body
- If you are able to, feel the chakra system, especially your second (lower abdomen) through throat chakras.
- Gently gaze outward until you see your "body double"– or an energy that is right around your physical body like a second skin
- As you sit with your etheric body, allow for yourself to feel the electrical sensation of it
- If you are able to visualize it, see this body as a bunch of electrical energy, or a grid– and not just a dark shape mimicking your physical body
- Now look out approximately six to twelve inches or so. This is typically where your astral body is, although some variance is to be expected
- This should look like an oval surrounding our physical body and etheric body. This is viewed by many as clouds, watercolors, or many colors swirling

- Sense or see to the best of your abilities this oval or the clouds or colors
- Now, again look for this body to be composed of a grid or having an electrical nature
- As the etheric and astral bodies span out, as you focus on them they will seem to twist, at the same time getting much larger and forming the varying other bodies, but at the same time getting smaller and forming a tunnel, or cord-like structure
- Many people report a blackening of vision as they reach this stage and a sort of head-rush or headache. If this happens, stop for the day and hydrate yourself
- If the blackout does not cause you to feel ill, you will simply sit and wait to full see the cord or tunnel
- As it comes into consciousness it will turn from a black or white image to a distinct, strong silver cord reaching out from your body into the distance. Although this cord can appear anywhere, it has been reported by those able to find it between the heart and solar plexus area, although it will not be felt within the physical body like some cords are
- When you are ready bring your consciousness back to your physical body. Open your eyes if they were closed, and feel your feet firmly on the floor

Typically sitting with and sensing this cord is enough to receive profound spiritual insights. There is nothing to "do" with this cord than to directly experience it. If we choose to travel, it will naturally be much easier through the discovery of this cord, even if we do not technically utilize it by other astral travel methods.

Although I encourage you to explore other methods, books, and teachers for traveling, you can travel utilizing the realization of the cord:

- When you focus on the silver cord, hold in your mind the cord as well as the "body" (etheric or astral) that you wish to utilize for travel
- With the realization of the cord in mind, allow for yourself to see an oval or opening going over the cord
- You will then visualize yourself walking on top of the cord with this body. You will see many doors you can enter to your right and left
- Remember how far you have walked down the top of the cord approximately and how many doors you have passed as you choose a door to enter
- Mark the door in some way on the inside and outside
- Enter the doorway and explore, ensuring that you keep careful track of how to get back to the door
- When ready to leave go back through the same door, walk along the top of the cord, and allow for whatever "body" you have utilized to grow larger and naturally take its correct place in your energy body

Although some people claim to be able to choose doors, or travel wherever they want at will, it sometimes is not clear enough for us to do so. Many of these people also have vivid imaginations, and while the mental process of doing this work can certainly garner benefits, it is much different in terms of impact and spiritual realization to actually have direct experience of it. What I am saying is that while you choose to travel you may wish to go to a certain place, but it never is with 100 percent certainty that that is indeed where you will end up. Certain people are more talented at traveling out of body than others, and they will likely pick this up because they have a specific knack for it. For many of us it may take a while, so we should have patience.

The typical rules and cautions apply. If we are not able to find a friend to ensure our safety, we should set an alarm clock to bring us out and back to our physical body. It is vitally important that we do not walk through the cord, but rather walk on top of it. Because this cord is the death and birth tunnel, we may find ourselves in an odd situation that no spiritual practitioner can help us with if we do walk the length of the tunnel. We may also find ourselves having a physical reaction if we do so, such as migraines, nausea, and stomach aches. So keeping ourselves on top of the silver cord, and not within it, is a way to explore that is much less likely to give us a head rush, or cause for us to go into a spiritual crisis of needing to mentally assimilate the information we have received.

For further information on how to travel appropriately, I do suggest a solid spiritual teacher who is experienced in this area. It can be very important while doing this work to ensure that you are fully back in your physical body, and to recall any energy that you may have scattered or left behind due to traveling to your physical body.

**How to Work with Your Mental Cord**
Similar to the Astral/Etheric silver cord, we have a cord that is focused on our mental body. Our thoughts, ideas, and insights come through this cording mechanism. Working with this cord can be wonderful for clearing our mind when we have too many thoughts, or for sensitives who pick up the thoughts of others easily.

When we have naturally reached a certain level of spiritual attainment our thoughts will naturally decrease, specifically the cyclic thoughts that most of us experience constantly. This effect of a clear mind is typically found through long-term meditation and spiritual practices, provided that we have not gotten stuck in our path.

But we can further train our thoughts as well as learn how to see and work with the pervasive field of thoughtforms– the multitude of thoughts creating an energetic field and energetic forms that surrounds us. The field of energetic thoughts is vibrant, electric, and surrounds us thickly. It is one of the most pervasive energies that surround us, and we rarely give credence to it since we are so focused on more basic energetic work.

This cord is, not surprisingly, located through the third eye area. Similar to the third eye chakra, it has a front and back aspect. It comes through the center of the forehead but also goes through the brain itself and exits out of the back of the head– basically where the top of the neck meets the back of the head and has an indent.

This cord is electrical and again will be more of a tunnel shape, corresponding to the third eye chakra. When our third eye is open, we are able to see the sheer amount of thoughts that surround us. These look like lines, cords, electrical matter, and occasionally clouds or other formations. The initial opening of the third eye and ability to see this short, dense, and electrical cord will allow for us to expand our vision into being able to see the energy of thoughts that surround us. It is through the viewing of this that we can be able to take responsibility for our own thoughts because we begin to realize the impact of them, as well as be able to work with the thoughts of others. There is also the opportunity to shape thoughts into specific images, such as is done with creating servitors.

As with any meditations being taught, even for the third eye, which is considered to be a largely visual chakra, being able to see psychically is not completely necessary. Employing our other senses, such as impressions we receive, our felt sense, and our gut instincts, will garner more information than we thought possible. It is by having confidence in the impressions that we receive, even if they are not outright visions, that we can progress spiritually in the way that is right for us.

With all that in mind, we will gently focus on the third eye area where it appears between, and in some cases slightly above, the eyebrows.

- Get a sense of the "front" of the chakra– the area from the skin on your forehead going outwards
- Now, get a sense of the "back" of the chakra– the area going from the back midline of the skull where it meets the top of the neck going outwards behind you. You are likely to perceive this at a bit of an angle
- Now you will feel these two areas connected– a cone of energy or light going from behind the back of your skull, through your brain, and out through your forehead. Sit with the visual or felt sense of this for a bit
- Now allow for this cone of light to fully illuminate your brain. Just sitting with this cone of light will do this without any forcing or "doing" necessary, but this may take a while if you are not able to sense the front and back of the chakra connecting

Out of the front of the third eye chakra is generally where we are able to see and sense the energetics of thoughts already out in the world. The back of the chakra is where we are more likely to pick up the thoughts of others currently. Although telepathy is definitely the sort of ability that cannot be cultivated by everyone, the ability to sense what other people are thinking (without hearing their actual thoughts) or even the ability to sense what their true nature is (who they are behind the mask that they are wearing for the world) is developed through the back of the third eye center.

In some people this area can grow quite large, and the entire back of the neck can be a receiving area of thoughts from others. Additionally, the back of the neck is an area where we are likely to get spiritually wounded– either by arrows or the projected thoughts of others gossiping or talking behind our backs. Having the ability to open this area and to cultivate it allows for us to more readily understand who is talking behind our backs and to sense the types of people who wear masks that are quite different than how they truly are. It can be a jarring realization to understand that the most "love and light" individuals are wearing a mask barely obscuring their passive-aggressive nature, their rage, and their grief, or that someone who you thought to be a friend is gossiping about you. In a positive manner, this center allows for you to see and realize "truth", and to appreciate it when you come across it in others.

When you are ready you will be able to sense this different information from the front and back of the chakra:

- Sit with the front aspect of the chakra and sense anything you are able to by looking outward through it
- Sit with the back aspect of the chakra and do the same

- Through the front aspect of the chakra sense or see a short cord or small tunnel-like structure. You will do this by simple, gentle focus to the area
- If you are able to see or sense this, you will follow it out. It will shortly expand into a large field, filled with electricity, clouds, and other objects. These are the thoughts of others
- If you are able to, look at your now illuminated brain and sense energy going through the third eye and entering this field of energy
- As you sit with both this field of thoughts as well as your own being siphoned into the field, you will begin to understand how much this field has an impact on you
- When you see or sense a shape repeating in this field, ask your gut intuition what this means. Repeat again for any other shapes or similar energies you see in this field. Gradually you will come up with a library of realized thoughts and thoughtforms
- When you notice yourself contributing thoughts that are of a nature that you do not feel is appropriate, take responsibility for them by returning to the sense of the light of the third eye chakra and sending pure white light from that chakra into the form that you have created

It is by taking responsibility for our own thoughts that over time we can have a clear mind. When we begin to recognize and categorize the shapes we receive or see before us we will begin to instinctively realize who these thoughts are coming from, what the thoughts are about, and what emotions are attached. It is in many ways much easier to navigate this world with these realizations. When we open this center we can look at individuals and see or sense the shapes and electrical emanations from them. This will allow for us to understand their true nature, as well as practically allow for us to perhaps choose another bus seat than one we might have chosen if we had not had this growing faculty.

When we are ready we can work with the back of the chakra. I suggest working with this one more simply. In most "sleeping" or unawake individuals this area has a cord or projection of some sort appearing to come from the outside penetrating it. Many describe this as a cord, however others describe this as a sort of tentacle, straw-like structure, or simply a rock or boulder. When we are ready we can "unplug" or detach this cord from us by asking the correct spiritual helper to do so. This may take many months, as this again is a sort of spiritual initiation that will allow us to see or sense a much greater spectrum of the world and universe than we once did. We may need to work at changing the cord, dissolving parts of it, or simply realizing that it is there for a period of time before we are ready and willing to let ourselves fully "unplug".

When we are able to unplug we may choose to create an energetic cap, shield, or many choose to actually wear an item of clothing that has been attuned to reflect or keep safe this area of the body. Although it seems odd, and is a funny sight, some shamans in ceremony will wear tinfoil over this area of the body for protection for the purposes of reflecting energies and thoughts. I am generally less of the tin-foil sort, so I have a talisman that I wear around my neck for the purposes of protection and reflection of any negativity, jealousy, or thoughts seeking to attach to me or attack me.

It is through the direct experience of these areas of the body gradually unfolding that we can have full usage and realization of them. Although I realize that this material is presented in such a way as if you follow several steps you will be in full realization, or in full realization of a particular cord or spiritual process, that is very rarely what happens. A gradual method is much healthier when approaching such deep spiritual and energetic anatomy. If we do something like remove the natural blockage at the back of the neck too quickly we may not be able to properly integrate the amount of increased spiritual stimuli coming our way. Likewise, if we launch too quickly into third eye practices we may have an existential crisis (as many do) about how fake people are. It is best to be gradual in these practices and approach them over time so that we can integrate them properly.

## Birth Cord to Mother and In-Utero Experiences

In your mother's womb there are two things that link you physiologically to your mother– the placenta and the umbilical cord. The placenta links you to the uterine wall in order to absorb nutrients, excrete waste, and provide for gas exchange through the mother's blood supply. This is then transferred to the baby through the umbilical cord.

In spiritual anatomy the placenta is considered a veil between the worlds. It is a boundary between life and death as well as many other worlds. The umbilical cord not only is responsible for physiological exchange with the mother but also energetic and spiritual exchange. In simple terms, this means that the emotional state, stressors and other issues going on in the life of your mother while you were in utero energetically created your beliefs of this world. Our experiences in utero create the basic primal energetic state most of us remain in for the rest of our lives.

So what does this mean? It means that if your mother was highly stressed during her pregnancy it is likely that you will be highly stressed or constantly in "fight or flight" throughout your life without knowing why. It means that large emotions, such as grief, anger, or depression that came up throughout the pregnancy can be a strong part of your energetic anatomy without you knowing why. It means that ancestral energies, traumas, and beliefs can come through to you. Basically, what this means is that the energetic, spiritual, and emotional environment you were corded to during your time in utero is likely to not only color your existence but has created it.

A large issue that comes up through the in utero experience is the desire to be present on Earth or not. This is based on if our mother in fact wanted us, or perhaps was ill or depressed during her pregnancy. In reaction to this we may have felt unwanted here on Earth. If there was fighting and stress during the pregnancy we may have created a false belief that the Earth is full of fighting and stress and that we wanted no part of it. If we were not properly given the right nutrition or ability to thrive we might not have fully decided to be here energetically. There also are many spiritual reasons why we may not fully incarnate or decide to fully inhabit our bodies that all happen in utero.

The time in utero is one of the first formative times where we are not only passed down the beliefs and experiences of our mother, and of our familial and ancestral lines, but is also how we develop our first impressions of this world. If we were in a safe, healthy pregnancy where we were fully loved and wanted we may go through life (barring any trauma after birth) as secure, confident individuals who feel safe in this world. If we were not part of a safe, healthy pregnancy– either physically, emotionally, energetically, or spiritually– we may feel unsafe in this world.

These are all primal instincts that were developed in utero and we have likely unknowingly acted out many times since our births. Although not a part of this cording course, the way that we were delivered, our first breath (or taking in of energy from the outer world and believing that the world can and will sustain us), and our formative experiences as an infant and young child are very important to our development. If you find that you do want to work with some of these things, finding an experienced CranioSacral therapist, a spiritual worker experienced in this type of work, or someone who focuses on breathwork can help you to release negative experiences of your first breath, delivery, or life after birth.

But for now we will focus on the tremendous amount of clearing and healing that can happen through working with the placenta and umbilical cord:

- First, sit and gently focus on the area of your navel
- To get to an in utero type atmosphere you will first allow for yourself to close your eyes and gently imagine yourself floating on a stream
- In this stream you will visualize a cord going into your navel and extending outward into the stream
- As you sit with this cord the stream will become an ocean, and you will be floating in it under water with your cord attached extending outward
- Imagine yourself in that ocean, feeling whatever emotions or experiences arise
    - Do you feel comfortable and at ease?
    - Are any strong emotions coming up?
    - Do you feel as if you are struggling for breath?
    - Are you able to let yourself float in this ocean, under water, without struggling– confident that you are being held and protected?
- As you ask these questions note any emotions that come up. If they do, that is okay. Simply allow for them to rise and release from you

- Next you will focus on the cord
    - What does it look like?
    - Does it seem healthy?
    - Are there any areas that seem imbalanced, stuck, or not flowing?

You should be able to feel a strong, clear flow of healthy loving energy coming towards you through the cording mechanism. Most importantly, you should feel safe, held, nurtured and wanted:

- When you focus on your experiences overall in this ocean do you feel a sense of being wanted?
- Do you feel held?
- Do you feel loved?
- Do you feel safe?
- Do you feel like you are getting the proper nutritional support?
- If you are not feeling those things, ask yourself what would happen if you could feel those things now?
- Let yourself experience feeling wanted, held, safe, and with the proper nutrition

If you have never experienced those things you may not wish to receive them fully at first. Allow yourself to receive whatever you are willing to at this moment– you can always go back and do this again and again to receive more.

In rare situations, you might find that you are really unwilling to receive anything, or there will be thoughts or experiences that arise concerning even wanting to be born, or to be on this Earth. It this happens ask yourself while still visualizing yourself in that ocean:

- What would happen if I did fully incarnate?
- What would happen if I decided I wanted to be here on Earth?
- What if it was my choice to be born?
- What do I fear by choosing to be here fully?
- Can I accept that I am here?

The answers to these questions can be enormously revealing as well as emotional. Allow yourself some time and space to reconcile what has come up for you. This is not an easy topic to broach– there are millions of us who have had similar issues and are walking around not fully embodied due to them.

If you are ready to fully incarnate, to choose to be here on Earth, you will go back to the previous section to receive the support and nurturing you need. Once you have received that, you will simply state that you are willing to fully be here on Earth. You will then have a spiritual helper reach out and hold the version of yourself in utero and bring it back to your current self, merging it into your heart area. If this is something that you would like help with, contact a spiritual worker who is familiar with soul retrieval to do so for you.

On rare occasion we had such a difficult, traumatic experience in utero that we just cannot receive the sustenance or support we need from our birth mother. She may be so imbalanced, toxic, or have such large issues that the psychic bond between the two of you is creating issues for you. This is not a step to take lightly, but in rare cases we may need to spiritually disconnect from our birth mothers to receive the type of safety, support, and nurturing we need to accept being here on Earth.

In this case you would again allow yourself to be in the ocean, but instead of that cord simply going outward it will go upward and connect to a "spiritual mother"– a figure in our own cultural pantheon of deities or archetypes that can give us the proper mothering that our own mother was unable to. You would do this by asking the energy or archetype of the spiritual mother you have chosen to step forward, and then ask them if they are willing to be a spiritual mother to you. You would then ask for them, or another spiritual helper, to attach your cord to their energy field (or wherever they say is appropriate) for the type of safety, sustenance, and support you need to fully decide to incarnate.

I will again repeat that this is not a step to be taken lightly, or a random choice to be made of spiritual mother. The psychic bond between mother and child, even if they have never met after birth (such as in adoptions or abandonments) is so strong that sensitives are able to pick up on emotions and experiences of their mother throughout their life. Likewise, picking and cording to a spiritual mother means that this is someone that you feel completely safe with and will receive guidance, support, and love from through that strong energetic bond. It is important that you feel strongly connected to a spiritual mother before you decide to cord to her.

In most of our cases sitting in this ocean while asking questions of the amount of support we feel is enough to create strong emotions and have other questions arise. It is also likely that we may not feel worthy of the amount of love and support that we require if we have never experienced it before. It is by the surrender to such support that we may receive it, and this will allow for the negative experiences, emotions, and beliefs that were created through this strong energetic cord to rise and release.

# About the Author

Mary Mueller Shutan is the Author of *The Spiritual Awakening Guide: Kundalini, Psychic Abilities, and the Conditioned Layers of Reality* published by Findhorn Press. She is also an Acupuncturist, Herbalist, CranioSacral Therapist, Zero Balancer, Energy Worker, and Spiritual Healer. Mary has helped hundreds of people worldwide navigate their spiritual awakenings and psychic abilities through her email based programs, Skype/Phone consultations, and distance Spiritual Healing services.

She can be reached via her website: www.maryshutan.com

Printed in Poland
by Amazon Fulfillment
Poland Sp. z o.o., Wrocław